The
Reiki
Bible

The
Reiki
Bible

THE DEFINITIVE GUIDE TO THE ART OF REIKI

Eleanor McKenzie

Bounty
BOOKS

First published in Great Britain in 2009 by
Godsfield, a division of Octopus Publishing Group Ltd

This edition published in 2011 by Bounty Books,
a division of Octopus Publishing Group Ltd
Endeavour House, 189 Shaftesbury Avenue,
London WC2H 8JY
www.octopusbooks.co.uk

An Hachette UK Company
www.hachette.co.uk

ISBN 978-0-75372-134-6

A CIP catalogue record for this book is available
from the British Library

Printed and bound in China

All reasonable care has been taken in the preparation
of this book, but the information it contains is not meant
to take the place of medical care under the direct
supervision of a doctor. Before making any changes in
your health regime, always consult a doctor. Any
application of the ideas and information contained in
this book is at the reader's sole discretion and risk.

Contents

Introduction

Reiki is a very personal practice. Your journey with Reiki will not be the same as mine. Your experiences will be different and the methods of practice you have been taught may vary from those described in this book, yet we are all practising the use of the universal energy known as Reiki. In my view, these differences can serve to make the Reiki community stronger if we remain open to the possibility that – while we all use the basic system as the foundation of our practice – there are many ways to utilize this universal energy, and that we can all learn from each other.

ABOVE Each of us makes a unique journey with Reiki yet we are all using the same universal energy.

Reiki has been a part of my life for 16 years, and I am profoundly grateful that I found it – or it found me – and for the changes it has made in my life, and the opportunities it has brought me to be of service to many wonderful people. That is why it has been such a pleasure, and an honour, to write this book and share my knowledge and experiences with you. In doing this, I am also indebted to the knowledge of others who have devoted themselves to increasing our understanding of Reiki and to promoting this powerful system of healing, the beauty of which is in its simplicity. Indeed, for me, Reiki is the embodiment of 'less is more'.

I don't set much store by rules, traditions and lineage. I received my First and Second Degrees from teachers of the Usui Shiki Ryoho, but when I felt the pull to take the Third Degree I was strongly drawn to the teaching of Diane Stein and found a student of hers to attune me as I was unable to travel to her. I am thankful to all of them. So, I am not a teacher or practitioner of a particular tradition, and you will find that reflected in my approach. What is of paramount importance to me is the Reiki energy and the intention to use it for the benefit of our own lives and those of others. This is the message at the heart of this book and, regardless of the tradition you come from, that is what unites us.

About this book

This book is about working with energy through the system of Reiki. Some will feel pulled towards Reiki as part of a personal spiritual practice, while others may focus more on the healing aspects of the system. Everyone must make their own journey with Reiki. There are as many paths to enlightenment as there are people. Reiki is just one of those paths, and each person who practises it will walk the path in their own way. One thing is certain – the person who practises Reiki has unlimited access to the life force energy for their own healing, and is also a channel for transmitting this energy to others.

The book aims to be as comprehensive as possible in the information it covers. I have tried to be objective and present Reiki in a way that people of all schools and traditions can relate to. I hope it will be equally useful to those who are new to Reiki as well as to those who are experienced practitioners.

BELOW Reiki offers us unlimited access to the life force in order to heal ourselves, and to heal others.

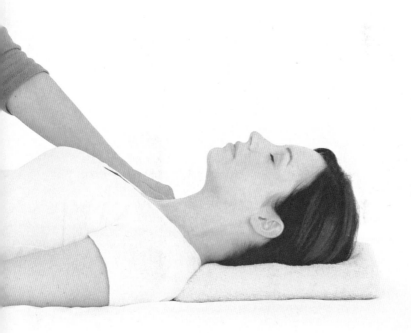

PART 1
The origins of Reiki

Energy

The Universe is energy. Out of energy everything is created. The energy your body is created from is the same as that of a mountain. It may seem incomprehensible that an object that appears to be lifeless and unchanging could have the same origins as a plant that is living, growing and constantly developing, yet that which is fragile is from the same source as that which is dense. This energy unites the Universe.

Universal life force

The concept of a universal life force can be found in a number of Eastern traditions. In Indian Ayurvedic medicine and in yoga it is called *Prana*; in traditional Chinese medicine, which is based on Taoism, it is called *Chi* or *Qi*, which then became *Ki* in Japanese. In the Christian tradition, it is accepted by some that references to *Light* allude to the same notion. According to Mantak Chia in his book, *Awaken Healing Light of the Tao*, this life force can be defined as energy, air, breath, wind and vital essence. In short, it is the activating energy of the Universe. When this energy is removed from a body or a plant, life has departed.

Although other cultures have long accepted the idea of a universal energy, or life force, that permeates everything,

Western culture has been more reluctant to accept such an idea. First, beliefs about the nature of the Universe were strongly influenced by a religion in which humans were superior to the rest of Creation, and the concept of a God who created the world but who 'lived 'outside it. Second, as science developed, and the idea of God became more questionable in many minds, people demanded proof before an idea could be accepted.

Over the last 50 years, physicists have been investigating matter, and have come to the conclusion that underlying all matter, in all forms, is energy. This energy vibrates at different rates, and it is because of this that a rock is more solid and dense than a human body. The idea that everything is formed from one energy source is very important when it comes to working with energy, whether through Reiki, Tai Chi or other forms of energy work. If everything in the Universe is created from one source, then all things, animate or inanimate, are connected. This means that we are constantly interacting with and influencing each other as though we were one gigantic body.

RIGHT One of the wonders of the world is that everything is created from the same universal life force: trees, mountains, oceans, machines and human beings.

Working with energy

Although the energy of the Universe is unlimited, within living creatures it is not. In the Chinese practice of Chi Kung (or Qigong) it is believed that we are born with an abundance of energy. When we are young, we are able to replenish our energy reserves; as we get older, we use up energy but are unable to replace it with the same ease. The result of this is a lack of energy, which can cause ill health, or a loss of the ability to live to our real potential.

Working with energy to reverse, or at least mitigate, this loss of energy can be found in a number of practices. For example, Chi Kung teaches that through practising a series of movements we can cultivate energy and bring ourselves back into a state of balance. In yoga, the breathing practice called *Pranayama* produces the same result. With the practice of Reiki, the energy is drawn from the Universe and transmitted through the palms of the hands to achieve a rebalancing of life force. Being in this state of balance enables us to enjoy life, to find contentment and to sense our connectedness to everything around us.

It is then to spiritual traditions such as Taoism, Buddhism and Hinduism that we must look for the physical and mental practices that will teach us about energy work, and its power to heal our own lives, and the lives of others. It seems ironic that Jesus is considered by many, and not just Christians, to have been the greatest healer, and yet for almost 2,000 years nobody listened to what he said about healing, believing instead that it was a divine gift available only to him. Yet Jesus clearly said, when he baptized the apostles with the Holy Spirit (which seems remarkably similar to the form of energy attunement used in the teaching of Reiki), that everyone could heal as he did.

It must be pointed out that working with energy is not about having a belief in God, or any religion. Working with energy can simply come from the desire to improve your life in all ways. It can be combined with a spiritual practice, or it can be a form of spiritual practice itself.

ABOVE Being in a state of balance, as symbolized by Yin/Yang, enables to us enjoy life fully.

Basic energy exercise

If you are a complete novice to energy work, or simply wish to experience the reality of energy, here is a very basic way to experience energy as something we can feel and work with.

1 Raise your hands in front of you at just below eye level, with your palms facing each other and about 30 cm (1 ft) apart.

2 Slowly push the palms towards each other until they are about 15 cm (6 in) apart, then bring the palms back to their original position.

3 Repeat this several times, until you can feel the build-up of energy between the palms. When you try to bring your palms together, you should feel some resistance from the energy between your hands.

Reiki and the East

The origins of Reiki are deeply rooted in Eastern traditions ranging from Buddhism to the martial arts. Reiki is a distillation of the philosophies of these traditions into one unique practice.

How Reiki began

The origins of Reiki are complex, in that it is a system that could be said to be both ancient and modern. It is modern because it was only developed in the last hundred years or so, and ancient because its origins would seem to be in a variety of spirit-centred philosophies that are as ancient as those of Ayurveda or Chinese philosophy, namely Buddhism, Shinto and Shugendô (see pages 18–21).

Reiki was developed in Japan by a man called Mikao Usui, who drew on a number of significant influences, and it was taken to the West where it evolved further. At the same time, Japanese Reiki also developed, and the two branches went in different directions. Recently, Westerners have also 'rediscovered' the Japanese branch of Reiki, so there is now quite a diverse range of Reiki practices. This section of the book attempts to set out clearly the details of this rather complicated evolution.

What does 'Reiki' mean?

Let us look at the word Reiki itself. The first books about Reiki in English translated the two Japanese *Kanji* or pictograms that represent the word as meaning 'universal life energy'. The *Rei* was thought to signify 'universal, transcendental spirit or boundless essence'. The *Ki* represents 'life force energy', and is equivalent to *Chi* or *Prana* in its quality. It would seem, however, that a more accurate translation is 'sacred energy', and that the word is simply a respectful way of referring to *Ki*. Reiki is not some energy that is separate to the basic *Ki* of the Universe – it *is* the basic *Ki*.

Japanese roots

Although there are now many variations on the original practice of Reiki, the system is undoubtedly rooted in Japan. The energy that is used in the system is, however, universal, and common to the many systems that are based on energy work. Reiki as energy is not something different or special, but the *system* of Reiki is unique. To try to understand the origins of the system, we must look first at some of the traditional beliefs and philosophies that exerted an influence on the life of its founder, Mikao Usui, and then how he came to develop the practice in a rapidly changing Japan.

RIGHT The Japanese *Kanji* for Reiki (pronounced *ray-key*) may be translated as 'sacred energy'. This *Ki* is the basic energy of the Universe and is not another form of energy that is separate from it.

Traditional beliefs and systems

Traditional Chinese Medicine (TCM) can be traced back to The *Yellow Emperor's Classic of Internal Medicine*, which was written some time between 2697 and 2598 BCE. Similarly, the principles of Ayurveda, which means 'the science of life', were handed down during the Vedic period in India, which dates back to between the first and second millennia BCE. Considered by many to be a divine revelation of Lord Brahma, its philosophy and methods of treatment were first described in two of its principal texts, the *Charaka Samhita* and the *Sushruta Samhita*. Like Chinese medicine, Ayurvedic medicine is as alive today as it was several thousand years ago. With their roots in the spiritual philosophies of Taoism and Hinduism, both of these systems have an energy-centred approach using a variety of techniques to restore a person to wholeness.

In ancient Japan, Buddhism, Shinto and Shugendo were three major influences on people's spiritual life.

Japanese Buddhism

Buddhist practices vary between the Theravada and Mahayana branches of Buddhism. All Japanese Buddhist sects stem from the Mahayana branch. While they may focus on different scriptures, they often share practices such as the repetition of mantras in a disciplined way, as well as following various precepts, so that the practitioner gradually reveals their inner knowledge to themselves.

Tendai Buddhism was brought to Japan by a Chinese monk in the 8th century CE. Initially not very popular, it started to thrive under the patronage of the emperor, resulting in it being the dominant form of Buddhism practised by the upper classes in Japan for many years. Its doctrines are based on the writings of the *Lotus Sutra*, which is also the basic scripture of Nichiren Shoshu Buddhism, practised around the world today.

Tendai Buddhism, like many other religions, has an esoteric tradition within it that is practised only by the few, such as monks and nuns, and is generally inaccessible to the majority of followers. This tradition within Tendai is called *Mikkyô*, which means 'secret teachings'. The teachings are based on a lineage system, meaning students of *Mikkyô*, as well as learning the teachings and practices, also had to receive something called *Kanjō*. This is an initiation by a Master of the *Mikkyô* disciplines in the form of an empowerment transmitted to the student from the Master.

RIGHT Tendai Buddhism was one of the most popular forms of Buddhism amongst the Japanese upper classes.

Shinto

Shinto may be translated as 'the way of the gods'. It is the native religion of Japan, and has similarities with the belief systems of other indigenous cultures, such as Aboriginal and Native American. It has no founder, no sacred texts and a very loosely organized priesthood. Shinto is a curious mix of nature worship, divination techniques, shamanism and the worship of *Kami*, which are both gods and spirits.

According to Shinto creation stories, a divine couple gave birth to the

BELOW The worship of nature and of *Kami* took place at Shinto shrines and was used as a unifying force during cultural upheaval in the 19th century.

Japanese islands, and their daughter Amaterasu Omikami became the ancestress of the Imperial family, resulting in the emperor being considered a living God. It was only at the end of World War II that the emperor was forced by the American government to renounce his divinity.

The Shinto *Kami* are very different to the concept of deity found in other religions. Apart from Amaterasu, the Sun Goddess, *Kami* were thought to be found in nature; particular areas had guardian *Kami*, as did families, and they were also found in abstract creative forces. Shinto practices revolved around revering the *Kami* and keeping them happy. The art of origami comes from Shinto, and examples of this intricate skill are to be found at many Shinto shrines. Out of respect for the tree *Kami* that gave its life to make the paper, origami paper is never cut.

Following the Meiji Restoration, Shinto was made the state religion in 1868. Combining Shinto with Buddhism was outlawed in an attempt to cleanse Shinto of all non-Japanese elements. It was seen as a unifying force at a time when the country was going through major changes, and foreign influences were destabilizing the purity of Japanese culture.

Shugendô

Simply put, Shugendô was a method of developing spiritual powers that combined elements of Shinto, shamanism and Buddhism. Although no longer practised in its pure form, remnants of it are still present in Tendai Buddhism and in Japanese culture, especially in the reverence for sacred places, particularly mountains.

Some call Shugendô 'mountain Buddhism' because the monks who practised it were called *Yamabushi*, which may be translated as 'one who sleeps in the mountains'. Founded by En no Gyôja some time around 666 CE, Shugendô was a deeply ascetic practice, in which followers spent years isolated in the mountains, developing magico-spiritual powers to heal.

Anyone undertaking Shugendô training would have to remove themselves from everyday life to an isolated mountain retreat, go through extreme fasts, including living on a diet of pine needles, and subject themselves to physical trials, such as standing under freezing waterfalls for long periods of time. They also had to memorize Buddhist sutras and continually repeat mantras taken from the sutras. As with Tendai Buddhism, the *Lotus Sutra* was adopted as one of the main texts of the practice.

Mikao Usui and 19th-century Japan

The originator of Reiki, Mikao Usui, was born in 1865, at the beginning of the Meiji Restoration in Japan. For the previous 200 years Japan had been isolated from the rest of the world – foreigners, and particularly Christian missionaries, were banned, and the country was run on a feudal system by Samurai warlords.

This 200-year long isolation was, in effect, ended by Commodore Matthew Perry, whose superior military force enabled him to negotiate a treaty with the Japanese that allowed American trade with Japan. Where Perry led, other Western countries soon followed, resulting in a rapid change in Japanese society as the foreign influences filtered through, and the country began its ascent towards becoming one of the major industrial nations in the world.

The breakdown of traditional society

Prior to this social, cultural and economic revolution, the majority of Japanese had a belief system based on a mixed bag of elements from the indigenous religion, Shinto, combined with parts of Buddhism and Taoism, brought from its neighbour, China. As the country opened up to ideas from the West, and Japanese people started to travel, usually for business and education rather than pleasure, the traditional Japanese society, which was more formal and structured than any society in Europe or America, started to break down.

With this gradual collapse of the structure of a culture, and as a result the rules of daily life (which had remained unchanged for hundreds of years), many Japanese began to feel the fear that accompanies radical change. For example, in rural areas, where people often depended on their offspring to help them with a farm, it was no longer a certainty that children would follow the destiny their parents had mapped out for them.

The need for a spiritual system

As a result of this uncertainty, many Japanese looked to religion in some form to show them a way forwards and help them to cope with their feeling of alienation. It seems likely that this search within Japanese society for some form of rock to cling to was the inspiration behind Usui's decision to devise a system of spiritual development that would be accessible to all people, and that was not a religion. This system was Reiki.

RIGHT Mikao Usui was born in an era of great change for Japan, just as it was emerging from 200 years of isolation from other countries.

The life of Mikao Usui

Until a few years ago, knowledge about the life of Mikao Usui was non-existent. Now we know much more about him, thanks to the discovery of his memorial stone. This was erected by some of his students at his grave in the Pure Land Buddhist Saihôji Temple in Tokyo, and has been translated into English by the Japanese Reiki Master Hyakuten Inamoto. Added to this, Usui's own notebooks have now been translated, although they are not widely available yet. Further information about his life and his teachings have been gleaned from some of his original students, although, not surprisingly, there are few of them left, given that Usui's teaching ended in 1926, when he died from a stroke while travelling around Japan.

Childhood

Mikao Usui was born on 15 August 1865 in a village now called Miyamo cho, in Gifu Prefecture. His family was *Hatamoto* *Samurai*, which is a high rank within the Samurai system. According to a family shrine at his birthplace, we also know that he had two brothers and a sister. During his childhood, he studied with Tendai Buddhist monks, and studied martial arts, a normal practice for a child of his class.

Studies and career

From his memorial stone, we know that he was a keen student and an avid reader. He was interested in everything from medicine, history and psychology to the more esoteric arts of divination and incantation. He travelled to Europe and America and studied in China, and his career included a position as private secretary to a Japanese politician who became mayor of Tokyo. According to the information on his memorial stone, although he had exceptional academic abilities he seems to have had problems with making his way in the world and fell into difficulties that are unspecified.

'The Universe is me, and I am the Universe. The Universe exists in me, and I exist in the Universe. Light exists in me, and I exist in the light.'

Mikao Usui, quoted by Hiroshi Doi in *Iyashino Gendai Reiki-ho*

However, his students have written that, despite the challenges he faced, Usui never lost the courage or will to keep going and to fulfil his destiny.

Family life

He married a woman called Sadako Suzuki, and they had two children – a son called Fuji and a daughter called Toshiko. Unfortunately, neither of his children enjoyed long lives. His daughter died in 1935 at the age of 22, and his son in 1946 at the age of 38. While he was married, he became a lay Tendai priest. By remaining a lay member of this Buddhist sect, he was able to continue having a family life. Little else is known about his personal life apart from these few fragments, but thanks to his own writings and the memories of his students rather more is known about his spiritual life and the influences on him that were to contribute to his system of Reiki.

RIGHT The Chiba family crest below Mikao Usui's gravestone indicates he belonged to one of the most famous Samurai families.

Influences on Mikao Usui

Mikao Usui, known as Usui Sensei in Japan, developed the system of Reiki in order to provide a simple method for the individual to reconnect with their innate spirituality in a Japan where the values of traditional society had begun to break down (see pages 20–21). It was never his original intention to send a system of healing around the world. Healing with the hands was only one aspect of his original ideas, which were influenced by a range of traditional belief systems and philosophies.

The outstanding achievement of Mikao Usui was to draw on all these practices, some of which would take an average person some 20 years to perfect, and from them create a system of using Reiki that was accessible to everyone. It also seems apparent that Usui was not simply intent on teaching a system of healing, but a holistic system that could take the follower on a path to enlightenment without the constraints of organized religion.

Tendai Buddhism

Mikao Usui's family were Tendai Buddhists (see page 24), and the young Usui trained at a local Tendai temple. Later in his life, he became a lay Tendai priest, indicating an attachment to this form of Buddhism throughout his life.

As Usui had become a lay priest, it is almost certain that he had been taught the esoteric, or 'secret', practices of *Mikkyô*. Teachings about healing were later added on to *Mikkyô*, and elements of Shinto were blended into it, such as spiritual practices connected with sacred mountains, to form the esoteric Japanese tradition that Mikao Usui would have learned. It is appropriate then that his ultimate vision of Reiki as a system came to him on Mount Kurama, a place of spiritual legend.

The exoteric, or everyday, form of Tendai that Usui was also familiar with used mantras and mudras (symbolic hand or body positions) as part of its worship; these were further elements that Usui would incorporate into his Reiki system. With its concepts of lineage, the transmission of an empowerment, its teachings about healing, and the use of mantras and mudras, it seems very clear that Mikao Usui used this form of Buddhism as the foundation of his system for using Reiki, and that he intended to make something secret accessible to a wider population.

Understanding the relevance of this form of Buddhism, which was brought to Japan from China, is important in seeing the practice of Reiki as much more than simply a hands-on system of healing. One belief about humans found in Buddhism is that each of us has complete knowledge of our divine nature, but that we are disconnected from that knowledge and are unaware of our own Buddhahood. Moreover, we can also become *Bodhisattva*, or enlightened beings, during our earthly existence and help others to achieve the same state.

BELOW The mantras and mudras of Tendai Buddhism are reflected in Usui's Reiki system.

Shinto

Growing up in Japan, Usui could also not have avoided the influence of Shinto (see page 20). This is not a religion, but more a way of life in which every aspect of the environment is imbued with spirits or gods called *Kami*. The notions central to Shinto that everything has 'spirit', whether animate or inanimate, and that contact with nature brings us closer to knowing the source of creation were seemingly adopted by Usui for Reiki. The fact that it was a religion without texts or written laws must also have guided Usui to bring that kind of flexibility to Reiki.

No Christian influence

Although we know that Usui was familiar with Christian scriptures, it now seems clear that he was never a Christian, nor did he teach at a Christian school. Christianity is not an influence in the development of Reiki, at least not in the way suggested in the story told by Hawayo Takata (see pages 40–43). Instead, the main influences in the development of Reiki are decidedly Japanese in origin.

Shugendô

Usui was also influenced by a form of Buddhism called Shugendô (see page 21). A main feature of practising this Buddhism was going to mountain retreats. Such a mountain retreat was to play an important part in the creation of Reiki. Mount Kurama was one of the sacred mountains of Shugendô, and it was here that Mikao Usui undertook a spiritual retreat, including fasting, that led to his formulating a system for Reiki. His memorial stone states that he received 'divine inspiration' on the mountain, although it seems clear from recent research that this inspiration was not quite in the same form as the story spread through the West by Hawayo Takata (see pages 40–43).

Shugendô also includes two other elements that are integral to Reiki. The first is the use of hands-on or palm healing to treat disease, and the second is the repetition of mantras. In the West, the use of mantras within the practice of Reiki has not been developed, but it now seems apparent from information coming out of Japan that Usui intended the five spiritual principles or precepts (see pages 60–61) to be used in this way, as regular repetition of them helps to integrate them into your life and brings focus.

Samurai

Given that we are now aware that Usui was interested in a broad range of subjects and had studied with Buddhist monks and studied martial arts (see pages 24–25), it is no surprise that in developing the system of Reiki he drew on a wide range of influences, including poetry, which was an essential part of the education of all the Samurai class. Without overemphasizing the importance of his Samurai origins, it is impossible to ignore it, as this tradition must naturally have exerted an important influence on his life and thought.

The traditional Western view of the typical Samurai is usually one of a sword-wielding warrior and, while this is correct, the Samurai also prided themselves on being men and women who cultivated the mind and spirit. Members of this culture valued their ability to write inspirational poetry for any occasion as much as they respected the fearless pursuit of honour in battle. This combination of physical, mental and spiritual discipline is the ideal foundation for a life in pursuit of enlightenment.

LEFT Mount Kurama was one of the sacred mountains of Shugendō Buddhism used for mountain retreats. It was here that Usui formulated the system of Reiki.

Martial arts

Combined with his Samurai upbringing, his training in martial arts, while perhaps not apparently important, must have added another dimension to Usui's understanding of the way that energy works, since nearly all forms of martial arts go beyond the physical, in their traditional forms. The children of Samurai were taught martial arts from a very early age. If Usui had been born into a peasant family, he would not have been able to bring this influence to Reiki. Yet what could an art that is more associated with physical discipline and fighting techniques bring to a spiritual and healing art?

Usui trained in Aiki Jujutsu, which was taught by its founder, Takeda Sokaku, towards the end of the 19th century. Takeda had created this branch of martial art from his own family's practices, accumulated over centuries, and decided to make it available to non-family members. One of Takeda's most famous students was Ueshiba Morihei, who became the founder of Aikido.

Aiki is principally composed of many physical moves, and has been described as a method that allows the student 'to overpower the opponent mentally at a glance and to win without fighting'. However, practising Aiki also involves learning ways of harmonizing the *Ki*

in a way that teaches the student to experience an inner calm, along with control and use of their willpower that would enhance their everyday life. According to early students of Usui to whom recent researchers have been able to talk, Usui did include elements of his martial arts training in his early teachings.

It is also known that *Mikkyô* and martial arts at times cross-pollinated in Japan. Monks taught *Mikkyô* techniques to martial artists and even Ninja (unorthodox warriors trained in all aspects of martial arts, who now have a unique place in popular culture), and in return the monks were taught fighting techniques. Therefore, the idea of blending these two apparently contrasting approaches to working with energy would have been considered quite normal by Usui and his peers. When you consider that martial arts are about discipline and the ability to win without fighting by working with the *Ki* of an opponent, it seems perfectly logical that Usui would use elements of it, and indicates that he intended practitioners of Reiki to apply the same kind of discipline to their practice as that of the martial artist.

RIGHT Although the martial arts are seen as primarily physical they also teach students how to harmonize their energy and understand how energy works.

The Usui Reiki Ryôhô Gakkai

The Usui Reiki Ryôhô Gakkai simply means the Usui Spiritual Energy Healing Method. Its original members were primarily naval officers. It was probably the case that at the time the majority of Japanese men of a certain class, who would have been able to join this type of society, were in the military. There is some suggestion that the fact that the original members were in the military may have had some influence on the more practical, less esoteric, aspects of the system, such as having a set routine for the placement of hands on the body.

The society had three levels of teachings: *shoden*, *okuden* and *shinpoden*, which is the teacher's level, each consisting of a further six sub-levels. At each of these levels the students acquired new knowledge. This would seem to indicate a required degree of dedication from the student similar to that needed to progress through the levels of any of the martial arts.

From interviews with early students of Usui, we know that the first thing he taught them was the five spiritual principles or precepts (see pages 60–61). They were later taught meditation and

mantras, including the use of Japanese *Waka* (see pages 90–91). Today's focus on Reiki as a method of hands-on healing is quite removed from what Usui was teaching at the time he founded the Usui Reiki Ryôhô Gakkai in 1922, and he only added the practice of palm healing in the last years of his teaching, just before his death in 1926.

The Usui Reiki Ryôhô Gakkai still exists in Japan, although in much smaller numbers than in its early years, because the period during and following World War II affected the existence of this type of society within Japan. Members of the society have been sharing some of the older teachings with Westerners, although in Japanese culture teachings of this nature are respected as sacred and not to be shared in a way that disrespects them. Therefore, we may never know everything about Usui's original teachings in Japan, although we can be sure that he would be surprised at some of the changes.

In their book *The Japanese Art of Reiki*, Bronwen and Frans Stiene reveal that in interviews with a Tendai Buddhist nun, Suzuki san, a direct student of Mikao Usui, the only common element she recognized between what she was taught and what is being taught in the West is the name of Mikao Usui.

Reiki and the West

Reiki made its appearance in the West due to the determination of one woman, Hawayo Takata, who made Reiki her life's work after discovering it in Tokyo in 1935.

How Reiki came to the West

Chujiro Hayashi was born in Tokyo in 1880. Having trained as a doctor and surgeon, he joined the Japanese navy, and by 1918 had risen to the rank of commander. By the time he joined Mikao Usui's school in 1925 he had retired from the navy. This was less than a year before Usui's death. Hayashi was also joined at the school by a number of other retired naval officers, and it was this small group that carried on the work of the Usui Reiki Ryôhô Gakkai after his death. Hayashi however, went his own way.

Five years after the death of Usui, Hayashi broke away from the society to open his own clinic and school called the Hayashi Reiki Kenkyu Kai, which translates as Hayashi Spiritual Energy Research Society. Some research suggests that Usui may have asked Hayashi, because of his medical knowledge, to write a guide to the Reiki system of healing that was an expanded version of his own guide to treating particular conditions, and that it was Hayashi's guide that Hawayo Takata (see pages 38–39) almost certainly used as the basis of her teaching.

Chujiro Hayashi and Hawayo Takata

At Hayashi's clinic people came to be treated by him and his students. It was to this clinic that Hawayo Takata came for treatment in 1935. She initially stayed for six months of treatment, and then for a further year as a volunteer once she had persuaded Hayashi to teach her. He was initially reluctant, as although she had Japanese parents she had been born in the USA, and the system was not supposed to leave Japan (according to unwritten 'rules' stemming from Japanese culture, its isolation from the West and its religious mystery traditions). He later helped her set up a clinic in Hawaii in 1938.

Chujiro Hayashi's legacy to the West was the training of Hawayo Takata, and the setting up of the first clinic outside Japan. Without this, Reiki might never have reached the rest of the world. However, it does not appear to be true that Usui named Hayashi as his successor in the Reiki lineage, as Takata's story (see pages 40–43) claims. It appears to be true that Hayashi committed suicide in 1940. Takata's version of events is that he had a self-induced stroke. However, it is more likely that he committed ritual *Seppuku* (cutting the abdomen with a sword) because he did not wish to enter World War II, leaving one lone woman to bring Reiki to the West.

RIGHT Chujiro Hayashi not only carried on Usui's work after his death, he was also instrumental in bringing Reiki to the West.

Hawayo Takata

Born in Hawaii of Japanese parents in 1900, Hawayo Takata's destiny was to bring Reiki to the whole world. Even if the system of Reiki she taught was different to Usui's original teachings, the many hundreds of thousands of people practising Reiki around the world today would not be doing so if she had not decided to return to the USA after training with Chujiro Hayashi.

Hawayo Takata arrived in Tokyo in 1935 for an operation. She had been widowed early in her marriage, and had suffered a number of debilitating conditions such as asthma and gallstones. While lying on the operating table, she heard a voice telling her that the operation was not necessary. After discussions with the surgeon and another member of staff, she made her way to Chujiro Hayashi's clinic (see pages 36–37), where she was treated, and her condition improved rapidly.

Teaching others

Following her training in Tokyo she returned to Hawaii, where she set up a clinic that soon became very popular. Hayashi visited her here, and it seems likely that it was during his visit to Hawaii

that he made her a Master (see pages 186–197). She was his 13th, and last, Reiki Master. She continued to work in Hawaii, only bringing Reiki to the American mainland in the 1970s.

After she started to teach throughout the USA and Canada, she decided it was time for her to instruct others on how to teach the system, and she created her first Master student, Virginia Samdahl, in 1976. Before her death in 1980, she went on to create 21 other Masters, who were responsible for the initial spread of Reiki. This resulted in the explosion of a worldwide Reiki phenomenon.

The 'Westernization' of Reiki

With the benefit of recent knowledge about Reiki's origins, it seems fair to say that Hawayo Takata was both astute and determined in ensuring the propagation of Reiki. She was astute because she removed many of the intrinsically Japanese elements of Reiki – particularly the explicitly spiritual elements drawn from Buddhism – that she knew Westerners would have difficulty with. It would seem that she also deliberately Christianized the story of Mikao Usui (see pages 40–43), for the same reason. As her students said, she was an accomplished storyteller, who loved to adapt the truth to what was necessary at the time.

LEFT Hawayo Takata was both astute and determined in ensuring the spread of Reiki outside Japan, and she is at the heart of a worldwide phenomenon.

Takata's story of Mikao Usui

I relate here the story of the discovery of Reiki as told by Hawayo Takata because it is the version that most people are familiar with. It is also interesting to compare it with new information and observe the skill with which Hawayo Takata wove a tale that combined truth, magic and sheer imagination, which could be compared with the story of the quest for the Holy Grail.

In a Reiki class, the story is told by the Master as part of an oral tradition, which Takata encouraged. Therefore, the story will never be told the same way every time, and each teacher will place emphasis on different elements of the story.

When I first heard the story, I saw it as a tale that combined historical fact with symbolic spiritual elements. Now I know that the historical fact is not true – Mikao Usui was never a Christian teacher and never a doctor of any sort. However, I can accept this divergence from the truth as a means to serve a purpose at the time. Referring to Usui as 'Doctor' gave him the kind of respect in the West that his title of 'Sensei' gave him in Japan. As Takata realized, the respect implied by 'Sensei' would be completely lost on Westerners, whereas 'Doctor' would not.

This is my shortened version of the story, as handed down from Hawayo Takata through the Usui Shiki Ryôhô.

The story of the discovery of Reiki

Dr Usui was a teacher at a Christian college in Kyoto. One day his students asked him if he believed literally in the Bible. He replied that he did. His students then asked him if he could explain the miracle healings of Jesus. Dr Usui could not explain, so he set off to discover the answer to the question of healing.

First he went to the West, because it was where Christianity was most widely practised and studied in a theological college in Chicago. But he did not find the answers he was looking for. However, during his time in America he learned Sanskrit, the language of the ancient scriptures of India and Tibet.

He returned to Japan, and travelled around Buddhist monasteries, believing that he might find the answer in the *Lotus Sutra*. However, the monks he encountered were no longer interested in healing the body and were focused on healing the spirit. Finally, he approached a Zen monastery where the abbot agreed that it must be possible to heal the body, as Buddha had done, but that the method had been lost. Encouraged by the abbot's response, Dr Usui stayed

RIGHT In Takata's version of the story, the healings of Jesus inspired Usui to discover the mystery of healing.

at the monastery, reading the sutras in their original Sanskrit. Although he found texts that described the method of healing, he still lacked the information that would enable him to activate the energy and use it himself.

He went to Tibet to read scrolls that documented the travels of a St Isa, thought by some to be Jesus, but returned to the Zen monastery still without the knowledge he required. The abbot encouraged him to continue his quest and recommended that he go to a mountain retreat for a 21-day fast and meditation, a usual practice for monks.

Dr Usui chose Mount Kurama and collected 21 stones to serve as his calendar. Just before dawn on the 21st day he picked up his last stone and prayed for an answer. At that moment he saw a light hurtling towards him across the sky. The light struck him in the third eye in the middle of his forehead. He saw rainbow-coloured bubbles, and in them the Reiki symbols. As he saw the symbols, he was given information about each one, and its use in activating the Reiki energy.

Excited at finally having his answer, he ran down the mountain, and on his way

stubbed his toe. He was amazed to find that after a few minutes the bleeding stopped and the toe was healed.

The purpose of the story

The story continues with other tales of healing miracles, and Mikao Usui's work in the Beggars' Quarter of Kyoto, which is actually based on the work he did following the great earthquake in Japan in 1923. Takata created a parable out of it that was meant to impress on students the need to pay for classes and treatments. According to her story those beggars who received treatments without charge showed no improvement. Usui then realized that there needed to be an exchange of energy in some form in order for healing to take place. Society widely accepts money as that form of energy in exchange for services, although there are many other ways to exchange energy, such as bartering. Inaccurate the story may be, but it has drawn many thousands to learn Reiki and provided them with a sense of tradition that would not have existed without it. What the story does provide us with is the sense of 'divine inspiration' that was involved in Mikao Usui's quest to create a system of healing and spiritual practice that offers its practitioners everything that they need to live a more fulfilled life.

LEFT The *Lotus Sutra*, and other Sanskrit texts, provided descriptions of energy healing, but no information on how to activate the energy and use it.

Reiki Today

Reiki has spread like wildfire across the globe, and on its journey through East and West it has evolved to meet the needs of the diversity of people practising it.

Reiki in the West today

The understanding of Reiki, as we know it in the West, has been changing over the last 10–15 years. This is largely due to the research of three people: Frank Arjava Petter, Bronwen Stiene and Frans Stiene. These three Reiki teachers have dedicated themselves to uncovering the system of Reiki as Mikao Usui taught it in Japan. Reiki practitioners in the West have also been able to advance their understanding of the system by the willingness of some Japanese teachers, particularly Hiroshi Doi, to share the principles of practising Reiki according to the system of the Usui Reiki Ryôhô Gakkai, the organization set up by Mikao Usui in 1922 (see page 33), to advance the practice of Reiki in Japan.

There are many Reiki teachers and writers, other than those mentioned above, who have also been instrumental in advancing our understanding of Reiki. We owe them a debt as they have added a new dimension to our understanding of the practice and its potential as a holistic system, and enlightened us about the life of Mikao Usui and the origins of the system.

The inaccessibility of Japanese culture for Westerners, owing partly to the language barrier and partly to very different cultural customs (particularly regarding practices considered to be sacred), has made it difficult for outsiders to gain information – hence the value of those who have spent time in Japan, and of those Japanese willing to come to the West and increase our knowledge.

How we refer to Reiki

In the West we have, until recently, talked about Reiki as if it was the system, whereas Reiki is actually the energy that the practitioner transmits. So, when we talk about the origins of Reiki we are really talking about the origins of the methods of using the energy. It is, therefore, more accurate to talk about 'the system of Reiki'. However, for the purposes of this book, and because it is referred to as Reiki by the majority of people, the system will be referred to as Reiki throughout.

RIGHT A handful of Western teachers have been dedicated to advancing our knowledge of Reiki in Japan and in bringing Japanese teachers to the West.

Reiki in Japan today

When Reiki started to spread through the West, nothing was known about what was happening in Japan. Nobody had heard of any Japanese teachers, and there seemed to be an assumption that when Chujiro Hayashi (the man primarily responsible for Reiki getting to the West) died, having first passed on his method of teaching the system of Reiki to Hawayo Takata, the practice of Reiki in Japan died with him.

We now know this was not the case. It is true that the impact of the post-war years on Japan may have caused Reiki to fade into the background for a time and its teachers to keep a low profile. This is understandable within the context of Japan becoming a leading industrial nation, leading to a decline in interest in spirituality among the new generation – similar to what happened in the West.

However, as Reiki spread in the West, it was only a matter of time before teachers began to be curious about what was happening to Reiki in its country of origin. This, coupled with the desire to seek out the original teachings, eventually resulted in the re-emergence of Reiki in Japan, ironically, with the Western style of Reiki more widely practised than the original teachings of the Usui Reiki Ryôhô Gakkai, which is a very private society (see page 33).

Exchanging wisdom

One of the first Reiki teachers to explore what was happening was Mieko Mitsui, a Japanese Reiki teacher living in the USA. With the advantage of being able to speak Japanese, she returned to Japan, taking her version of Reiki with her. Others have followed in Mieko Mitsui's footsteps, both bringing Western-style Reiki to Japan, and, importantly, discovering what has been happening in Japan since Mikao Usui first started to teach his system. There have been surprises and revelations on both sides, as you might expect.

For the Japanese practitioners who trained with Usui and who are still living, there was the surprise of discovering that Reiki had left Japan, and was now a system practised by people in almost every country. For the Westerners, there was the revelation that Reiki was still being practised in Japan in its orginal form, just as Usui first taught it.

RIGHT In Japan, Reiki is practised in its original form as Usui taught it. However, the Western form is increasingly popular.

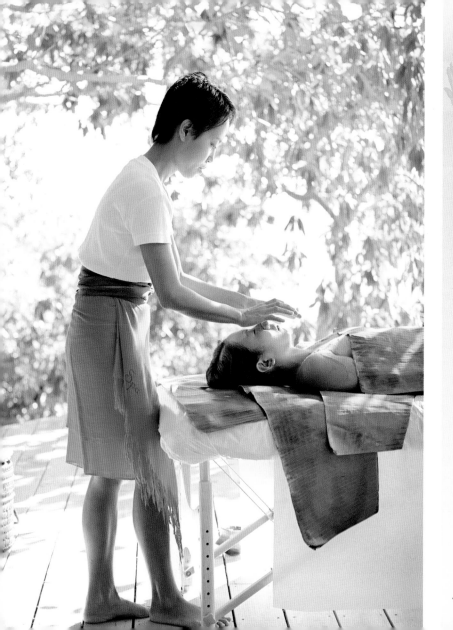

Reiki in the 21st century

Towards the end of the 1990s there was an almighty row happening in the world of Reiki. At the time, it seemed to me that the practice, the simplicity of which appeals to people from diverse backgrounds, was being turned into the type of sectarian battleground associated with organized religion. Letters arrived from Reiki Masters instructing students about what they should believe, and

arguments raged on the internet. Reiki had an 'us' and a 'them' – the traditionalists and the independents.

As is often the case, the faction identifying themselves as traditionalists felt that they were teaching the 'real' Reiki. Anything else was wrong. The publication of Diane Stein's book *Essential Reiki* was a prime bone of contention because it published the Reiki symbols,

an act that was anathema to members of the Reiki Alliance, the organization headed by the granddaughter of Hawayo Takata, Phyllis Lei Furumoto, who resigned from the Alliance in 1992.

Natural diversity

With the benefit of hindsight, we now know there have always been differences in the methods and teaching of Reiki. In Japan, Chujiro Hayashi's system differed from Usui's, and now other Japanese versions exist alongside the original Usui Reiki Ryôhô Gakkai (see page 33). Throughout the world there are innumerable schools of Reiki, and offshoots of it, such as Seichem.

In the West, when Hawayo Takata's Master students met after her death to discuss what they had been taught and how to teach Reiki, they discovered that she had taught many of them different techniques and that there were quite distinct differences between the symbols she had taught some of them. This is not surprising when you consider that there was a period of 30 years between Mrs Takata becoming a Master and her teaching Master classes herself, and that

no Master was permitted to write the symbols down. They had to be drawn from memory.

Feel the energy

Knowing that Mikao Usui created a simple method of accessing and using Reiki means that there never would be just one method. It was bound to evolve, because it is the energy, not the method that is most important. I know that there may be many people who will disagree with this, yet we know from experience that Reiki taught in different forms does work. It seems to me that it goes against the spirit of Reiki to declare that one method of teaching or practising it works better than another. Who are we to judge? Each practitioner will find the method that is most appropriate for them. Some will choose to follow more traditional methods while others are drawn to explore alternatives. Everyone has their own path and the right to be respected for the path they take. The most important thing is that Reiki continues to be taught and practised in a spirit of tolerance and love and with gratitude to Mikao Usui for the gift he brought to the world.

LEFT In the 1990s, living members of the original Usui Reiki Ryôhô Gakkai were surprised to discover that Reiki had left Japan and was being practised worldwide.

PART 2
Discovering
Reiki

What is healing?

The English word 'heal' comes from the Anglo Saxon word *hal*, which primarily meant 'whole', but it also meant 'healthy' and 'holy'. In modern times, these words have lost their connection to each other, just as Western culture has, for the most part, lost the connection between health and wholeness.

In Western medicine, it is generally accepted that there is no 'soul dimension' to disease. Disease originates in the physical body, or the environment, and treatment focuses on the body. The mind has come to play a bigger part in doctors' thinking about the outcomes of treatments; but, while they may accept that a positive attitude can influence the results of treatment, this is seen as a random effect rather than an integral element of the healing process.

With body, mind and spirit disconnected, there can be no complete healing. A soul that is sick will manifest its 'dis-ease' ultimately as physical symptoms. Alternative therapies diverge from conventional medicine in their understanding of the origins of disease. The therapist sees the patient as being more than a body. Therefore, they also seek to treat the spirit within, which is the key source of imbalance in our minds and bodies.

Becoming connected

Being healed is to become connected once more to the soul. This may not always result in a physical healing. It may be that the healing is such that it allows the person to approach the transition of the soul from the body in a way that helps them to understand their life, complete their journey and accept their imminent death. We should not, therefore, confuse being healed with necessarily being in good health.

At the heart of healing there is love and compassion. The act of wishing to heal yourself or another is an act of love and compassion. When we are disconnected from love, we become disconnected from others; when we are connected to love, we feel closer to people and to nature. Through love we become One. Through Reiki we can connect with love, and express it with compassion both to ourselves and others.

Reiki can help us to understand the root causes of any dis-ease that afflicts us. The thoughts and feeling we have about ourselves and the world are the chief cause of our suffering. Yet we must learn to explore these beliefs with compassion and without guilt, and without judging the people who gave us these beliefs, such as 'I am not good enough'.

'The cure of the part should not be attempted without treatment of the whole. No attempt should be made to cure the body without the soul...this is the error of our day, that physicians first separate the soul from the body.'

Greek philosopher Plato, 427–347 BC

ABOVE Plato believed that complete healing must have a 'soul' dimension and that the body, mind and spirit all needed treatment holistically.

ABOVE Meditation is a form of healing that helps
people to develop a connection with spirit.

Spirituality and Reiki

Spirituality and religion are not the same thing. A person who follows a religion may be spiritual, but not all religious people are spiritual. People tend to define themselves as spiritual when they want to communicate the fact that they believe in spirit as an important dimension of life, but don't follow any particular religion.

One of the simplest ways of defining the difference between religion and spirituality is that in religions followers look to a divine power outside themselves for help and healing, whereas those who follow the path of spirituality look to a power within themselves, that they may or may not call divine.

Healing that helps people to develop a connection with spirit is spiritual healing. This can take many forms – meditation, yoga and Tai Chi all do this, as do those methods in which the healer acts as a conduit for the life-force energy, such as Reiki. We can see here that in some forms of healing, such as meditation, the individual works alone, whereas with Reiki the individual works alone or with others. The important thing to remember is that all these forms of healing are focused on reconnecting with spirit. The difference is in the method.

Reiki, as it has been widely taught, is not connected to a religious practice, yet it is a spiritual path. It does not require belief in God or some form of higher being, but encourages each individual to seek the truth for themselves.

Influence of Mikao Usui

With the new information about the influences of various Buddhist practices on Mikao Usui (see page 25–29), and the elements he included in his Reiki system, we are aware that Reiki has a more religious dimension than was previously thought or taught. Yet it is clear that it was never Usui's intention to bring religious dogma to Reiki, but instead to free people from it, and at the same time provide them with a spiritual practice that would embrace diverse personal beliefs about God or the Universe.

Those who wish to now have the opportunity to incorporate practices into Reiki that Usui brought from *Mikkyô*, Shugendô and the martial arts. These, in my opinion, add a spiritual dimension to Reiki that makes it a complete system for spiritual enlightenment and takes it beyond an 'instant' healing method that focuses solely on channelling energy through the hands. To fully appreciate the benefits of Reiki, we must use all five elements of the system that have remained constant throughout all the changes that have taken place.

The five elements of Reiki

As we have discovered, Reiki has changed and evolved in many ways since Mikao Usui started teaching the system. It has been adapted to suit Western culture by Hawayo Takata, and, as even her students could not agree on one system, many others have introduced their own ideas.

Only five original elements remain that are common to Reiki everywhere. It is important for the system to identify these unifying elements, so that we have some sense of unity in our diversity. It is also these elements that make Reiki distinct from other forms of spiritual healing. The five elements are: *Gokai, Kokyû Hô, Tenohira, Jumon and Shirushi, Reiju.* Of these five, the practice of breathing techniques is not generally taught in Western Reiki classes, but those who are familiar with Chi Kung or yoga will know the benefits of breathing exercises in working with energy, so I have included breathing exercises in this section so that everyone can learn them.

Often the Reiki practitioner is not taught the importance of connecting all these elements together in one complete practice and, as I have said before, with 'fast-track' Reiki classes the emphasis tends always to be on the hands-on healing techniques, with elements such as the precepts being seen as of minor importance, or taught in a way unconnected to the hand positions.

In their book *The Japanese Art of Reiki*, Bronwen and Frans Stiene point

Japanese name	Western name
Gokai	The five spiritual principles or precepts
Kokyû Hô	Breathing techniques
Tenohira	Hands-on or palm healing
Jumon and Shirushi	Symbols and mantras
Reiju	Attunements

out that 'It is not the energy itself that makes this system unique, but the path that is walked'. Most of the five elements can be used alone, and most will only be used by the student working alone, the only exception being the hands-on healing, which can be used on others. It is clear that Usui intended students to use each of the elements systematically,

ABOVE By following a daily practice that is comprised of a number of harmonious elements, we find the path to enlightenment is made easier.

creating a daily practice that combined all five. Each element has its own lessons for the student, so by practising all of them the student has a fully rounded path to spiritual enlightenment.

The five spiritual principles

When I first learnt Reiki many years ago, I remember being taught that Mikao Usui had written a set of spiritual principles or precepts (*Gokai*) after he had worked in the Beggars' Quarter (see pages 40–43). This was part of Hawayo Takata's version of Usui's story. We were told that he had probably taken these guidelines for living a fulfilled life from a text written by the Meiji Emperor, while some teachers thought they came from his Christian beliefs. As we now know that Usui was not a Christian, that source can be discounted. While it is very likely that the precepts were influenced by the writings of the Meiji Emperor, they are in fact basically a non-religious form of traditional Buddhist precepts, such as those of the Eight-fold Path. The precepts are simply guidelines to living life well.

Whatever the source, I also remember that little emphasis was put on using the precepts as part of our Reiki practice. We were taught that reciting the precepts daily, or following one of the principles throughout the day, would have remarkable effects on our consciousness, but we were not taught a method of meditating on them. This was simply how Reiki was being taught, and the teacher was, at the time, unaware (as we all were) that Usui had put the spiritual principles at the centre of his system.

The importance of the principles

The precepts are the heart of Reiki. Mikao Usui wrote these as a guide to the spiritual journey. Everything else in the Reiki system supports these principles. It is these that the practitioners should meditate on every day in order to truly know what Reiki is and stay focused on it.

There are a number of variations on the principles taught, but this translation from Mikao Usui's notes by Chris Marsh (in *The Japanese Art of Reiki* by Bronwen and Frans Stiene), is, in my opinion, the most beautiful in its simplicity, and the closest to the spirit of Usui. Usui left these instructions for their use:

The secret of inviting happiness through many blessings, the spiritual medicine for all ills.

For today only:

Do not anger
Do not worry
Be humble
Be honest in your work
Be compassionate to yourself and others.

Do Gasshô every morning and evening, keep in your mind and recite. Improve your mind and body.

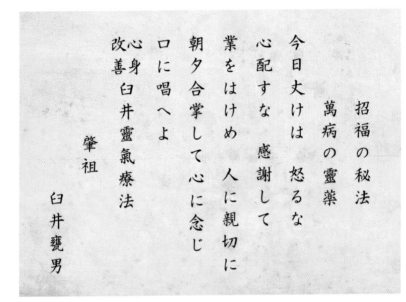

招福の秘法

萬病の靈藥

今日丈けは　怒るな

心配すな　感謝して

業をはげめ　人に親切に

朝夕合掌して心に念じ

口に唱へよ

心身改善臼井靈氣療法

肇祖

臼井甕男

Usui tells us first of all about the benefits we will receive from meditating on the precepts, which are happiness and relief from suffering whether it is of the mind, body or spirit. He follows this with practical advice about the position to meditate in (Gasshô) and suggests that you learn them off by heart so that you can recite them with ease twice daily. He then finishes by stating the ultimate aim of reciting the precepts, which is to 'improve mind and body'.

ABOVE This illustration of the five spiritual principles in Japanese may be used as a focus for a visual meditation on the precepts.

Meditative postures

In his brief directions (see page 60), Usui is saying that there are benefits to be gained from meditating on the five spiritual principles and following the Reiki system. He instructs the student to recite the precepts twice every day, sitting if possible in the traditional Japanese *Seiza* posture (see pages 78–79), with hands in the *Gasshô* position, both of which are explained and illustrated in this section.

Almost every spiritual practice has a number of postures that followers adopt, and Usui would have been influenced by both his Buddhist training and Japanese culture, which has a very precise body etiquette focused around showing respect. Other meditative postures (such as sitting in an upright chair, or cross-legged on the floor) may be used if you find the *Seiza* one too difficult, but the most important thing to remember is the *Gasshô* position.

The *Gasshô* position

Gasshô means 'to place two palms together'. Being in the posture brings the two sides of the body together. Keeping your hands in one position helps to still and focus the mind in meditation. It is also a way of showing respect for what you are doing. Use the *Gasshô* posture every time you meditate on the precepts, just as Mikao Usui instructed.

1 **In a kneeling, standing or sitting position, bring your hands up to the level of your heart and place the palms together as if in prayer.**

2 **Don't press the palms together tightly, but allow a little space between them, and keep your hands relaxed.**

Principles of preparation

These are to be followed when meditating on the spiritual principles and doing the breathing exercises.

- Know the technique or spiritual principle you are going to use
- Sit in *Seiza* (see pages 78–79)
- Release tension from the body
- Focus on the *Hara* (see pages 104–105)
- Place hands in the *Gasshô* position.

Spiritual Principle 1

Before meditating on each principle or precept, it is important to remember that Usui instructs us always to begin with 'For today only'. The purpose of this instruction is to keep us focused in the present. People in the West will have probably heard a similar instruction, 'Just for today', which is associated with the 'Twelve Step Programme' for treatment of addictions. Not only does the instruction keep us in the here and now, but it is also easier for us to believe that we can do something for one day rather than for long periods of time.

One writer who explains the idea from a slightly different perspective is Louise Hay, who tells us in her book *You Can Heal Your Life* that 'the point of power is always in the present moment'. Events in our life are created by thoughts and beliefs we have held over time. But they are all in the past and today we can replace them with thoughts and beliefs that create a happier life.

Do not anger

Always follow the principles of preparation (see page 60) when meditating on the spiritual principles and doing the breathing exercises.

For today only:
Do not anger

Part of meditating on this precept requires us to consider the nature of anger. No doubt painful memories will arise of times when we lost our temper or of when others were angry with us, and we felt our bodies shrink at the force of their fury. We try to avoid other people's anger, but we are sometimes less concerned about avoiding our own anger and feel free to unleash it at will.

Anger tends to arise out of the feeling that we have lost control of a person or a situation. When we become angry with another person, we feel that we are regaining that control. This is, of course, a false perception. We are actually losing control of ourselves.

If you observe your anger as it arises, you will see that it reflects something about you that needs attention, rather than a defect in the person you are angry with. Other people we draw into our lives are our mirrors, so look carefully at those who annoy you the most as they reflect aspects of yourself you would rather not see. Become an observer of your anger before you express it, then you will realize that there is nothing to be angry about.

LEFT When we unleash anger it is because we feel we need to regain control over others. But it is ourselves we have lost control of.

Spiritual Principle 2

It is a good idea to place a copy of the spiritual principles where you can see them every day, for example on your fridge. Alternatively, you could practise your handwriting skills and write them out on special paper; you could also add illustrations and put them in a frame. You may want to put the principles in several places around your home or keep them near you at work so that you are constantly reminded of them.

You can choose to recite the precepts out loud, or repeat them silently to yourself. The advantage of reciting them aloud is that you will be able to make a stronger connection with the meanings, just as chanting the mantras aloud helps you to benefit from the vibration of their sounds (see pages 88–89).

Do not worry

Always follow the principles of preparation (see page 60) when meditating on the spiritual principles and doing the breathing exercises.

For today only:
Do not worry

Worry is everywhere. Everybody seems to be worried about something, and some of us are champion worriers, seeing only dark clouds overhead no matter how brightly the sun is shining. Worry causes unnecessary stress, and when we worry about others we believe that worrying about them is a way of showing concern. But worry is not a demonstration of love; instead it is a manifestation of our inner fears directed at others.

Also, when we worry we are living in the future rather in the now. There is truth in the saying 'it might never happen', but when we worry we are pretty sure it will. Worry robs us of a peaceful mind, and is a waste of our time and energy.

When we worry we have lost faith. We are no longer able to see 'the big picture' or trust in what is happening to us. We worry about the future and try to control it in order to protect ourselves from pain, instead of allowing it to unfold gracefully and experiencing even greater things than we could imagine for ourselves.

Mostly we worry because we don't believe that the world is full of abundance, and we feel we will have to fight for everything we want. Choose something that is a worry for you, and just for today don't worry about it. Ask the Universe for help with it instead, and have faith that when you ask you will be answered. Don't waste time worrying.

RIGHT When we worry we are living in the future rather than in the present. Instead have faith that the Universe will support you.

Spiritual Principle 3

The principles are intended to help us live with correct attitudes. People who are advanced spiritually will have integrated these principles into their life, and these will be as natural to them as breathing. However, most of us need to be reminded about what we should be most mindful of. Some of the principles will resonate more with us than others, and it is instructive to be conscious of the ones you are drawn to most, and the ones you prefer to ignore. Ask yourself if it is perhaps the case that the ones you think you need to connect with least are in fact the ones that may require more attention in your life.

Be humble

Always follow the principles of preparation (see page 60) when meditating on the spiritual principles and doing the breathing exercises.

For today only:
Be humble

Being humble, or showing humility, unfortunately has a number of rather negative connotations in the English language. These might be the ones that come to mind when you contemplate

LEFT Gratitude is the essence of being humble. Wake up every day and be thankful for all you have.

this precept. A person who is described as being humble is considered to be modest, meek or self-effacing. It also implies being poor or underprivileged; and, perhaps worst of all, a humble person may be seen as subservient. These attributes are not highly thought of in a society that tends to value people who achieve at the expense of others, rather than those who put themselves at the service of others.

Therefore, we would rather not see ourselves as humble. In modern terms, it defines us as a 'loser'. Yet if we look at some spiritual leaders, philosophers and scientists, along with those who work for the greatest good of humanity, we will probably acknowledge that they share a quality of humility that allows them to let their gifts shine so brightly.

To be humble does not mean to indulge in false modesty or force yourself into self-effacing behaviour. This is a form of egotism. Instead, consider gratitude to be the essence of being humble.

When you wake up, say 'thank you' for your life and everything in it, no matter what, and the opportunity to experience yet another day. Gratitude to the Universe for both the good and bad aspects of your life, and of other people, brings you peace and abundance. Being humble means accepting the truth of your inner self and living that truth.

Spiritual Principle 4

When introducing the Reiki precepts into your life you might want to consider what principles you already use to guide your life. Are you truly conscious of them, and could you write them down? This is an interesting exercise as most of us believe that we have guiding principles, but we are unclear about what part they play in our daily lives, and we are perhaps less than honest with ourselves about the rules we live by.

Be honest in your work

Always follow the principles of preparation (see page 60) when meditating on the spiritual principles and doing the breathing exercises.

For today only:
Be honest in your work

This is perhaps the principle that people may have most trouble understanding. It would appear at first reading simply to refer to your approach to work, as in your job. However, I believe that it requires a much broader interpretation, and is asking us to take a look at how we conduct ourselves in all aspects of our daily life.

When looking for the meaning of this principle, ask what qualities associated with honesty are most important to you? You may consider honesty in speech and actions crucial regardless of how this affects other people. Is this type of honesty sometimes a form of egotistic pride?

Perhaps more than anything this precept asks us to be honest with ourselves. We are all too often dishonest with ourselves in lots of ways. We let ourselves off the hook for actions we hardly tolerate in others. We cheat ourselves and steal from ourselves when we neglect our Reiki practice, for example, or when we don't follow our passion in our work, and do what is expected of us instead. Consider your whole life as your work, and contemplate the areas where you could be more honest, and what you need to do to achieve this.

Mirror work

A practical method of working with honesty is doing mirror work. Look in the mirror and say out loud something that you admire about yourself, for example, 'I am lovable'. How does it feel? Did you feel any discomfort when you said it? Be honest with yourself, accept what you feel and change it if you need to.

RIGHT It is important for us to learn to be honest with ourselves before we can begin to be honest with others.

Spiritual Principle 5

Integrating the five spiritual principles into your life requires self-discipline in developing a daily practice. It also means accepting yourself with love. When you perceive defects, don't respond with guilt and shame. The shadow side, as some call it, needs to be acknowledged. We would prefer it not to exist, and treat it as the enemy. The more we continue to fight with this aspect of ourselves, the less chance we have of loving ourselves or others. You may want to write down some of your negative beliefs about yourself and ask yourself who gave you these beliefs, and whether you really have a reason to continue holding onto them.

Be compassionate to yourself and others

Always follow the principles of preparation (see page 60) when meditating on the spiritual principles and doing the breathing exercises.

For today only:
Be compassionate to yourself
and others

Note that first we are instructed to show compassion to ourselves. When we show ourselves love, we are more able to give love to others – but it is often difficult to love ourselves because there is so much we don't like. Acceptance and forgiveness of all that we find less than perfect in our lives is at the core of being compassionate.

Valuing the contribution that all other people make to our lives enables us to show them compassion. This includes those you perceive as causing problems, and those who make you angry or are the source of worries. Meditating on the divine purpose of pain as well as joy in life will enable you to become compassionate, and to be One with everything.

Affirmations
When we repeat an affirmation regularly we show ourselves compassion and a willingness to change for the better.

Consider what you want to change in your life. Dig deep to discover beliefs you hold that are preventing you from making that change, then write an affirmation that frees you from these beliefs. For example, if you feel insecure, you might affirm that 'The Universe always supports and protects me'.

LEFT When we love, forgive and accept ourselves it is so much easier for us to show compassion to others.

Breathing techniques

Breathing is fundamental to our existence. We can live without water or food for several days and still survive, but we cannot stay alive for more than a few minutes without breathing. At birth, the baby's first breath is also the first time it draws energy into its body that has not come through the mother. Air is a primary source of energy, and breathing is the mechanism of ingesting it, yet we barely give the process a thought, unless we have a problem with it. Nor do we consider the effect that breathing has on our other body systems – breathing is simply something we do until we die.

Both our state of mind and the state of our nervous system can have a profound effect on our breathing, and vice versa. When we are upset or anxious, we feel the chest tighten and our breathing becomes shallower and faster. Because our breathing is shallow, our body is not taking in enough oxygen, so we breathe even faster in the attempt to take in more. The extreme result of this is hyperventilation, which tends to cause dizziness or fainting, and is frequently associated with panic attacks.

Anxiety states also affect our ability to circulate *Ki* smoothly around the body, and to draw more energy into our bodies. By slowing down our breathing using meditative techniques, we can improve our circulation of *Ki* and increase the amount of energy.

In Japanese, the breathing techniques taught by Usui are called *Kokyu Ho*. Controlled breathing is found in both yoga and Chi Kung for self healing, and in martial arts for raising energy.

Exhaling

One of the first-aid procedures for dealing with a hyperventilation attack is to get the person to breathe into a paper bag so that it expands. The reason for this is that we need to exhale more when we are hyperventilating, even though our instinct is to increase our inhaling. This is why the exercises on the following pages place more emphasis on the out-breath. In the basic Chi Kung breathing exercise (see pages 76–77) the emphasis is on exhaling. It is this action that allows your body to relax. We even say that we 'heave a sigh of relief', when our breath reflects the mental release we are experiencing.

RIGHT Breathing techniques are invaluable in helping us to improve circulation of *Ki* and increase our energy.

Breathing exercise 1

This basic exercise from Chi Kung will help you to take slower, fuller breaths. Before you begin, you might want to find out how many breaths you take per minute. The average person takes about 16 breaths per minute, but after practising this breathing exercise regularly you should find that this is reduced to five or fewer. Beginners and anyone with breathing problems, however, should not try to force changes in their breathing. Just keep up the practice and the changes will occur naturally at a pace suited to you. Don't hold your breath at any time in an attempt to slow the breath down.

You might find it useful at first to place your hands on your abdomen or your chest so that you can feel the movement of your breath. You can practise this standing or lying down, or using the *Seiza* posture (see pages 78–79).

If you practise this technique regularly, you will find that you start to use this form of breathing naturally without having to concentrate on doing it.

1 Begin by exhaling through your nose. At the end of the out-breath, tighten your stomach muscles and flatten your stomach slightly. You will feel your diaphragm muscle push up as you do, squeezing the air up and out of you. Push as much air out as you can without forcing it, until you feel your lungs are empty.

2 Relaxing the stomach muscles, breathe in naturally and bring the air down into the abdomen so that it swells up under your hands like a balloon. Don't force this or you will create tension and spoil the effect. Once your abdomen feels full, exhale again, repeating step 1.

Caution

Don't practise this technique excessively at first. Start with three breaths at a time and gradually increase your number of repetitions.

1

2

Posture for breathing

Ki breathing improves delivery of nutrients around the body and accelerates the removal of toxins. It also strengthens the liver, kidneys and immune system. Our posture significantly affects the quality of our breathing. If you have asthma, or know somebody who does, you have probably noticed that during an attack there is a tendency to hunch the shoulders and round the back. This closes the chest area up, which results in constricting the breathing even more. Often the body keeps this posture even after the attack is over. This contributes to the continuation of the condition.

Opening up the chest area (by keeping the shoulders down and back, by regularly adopting the *Seiza* posture shown here, or doing exercises that stretch these muscles) is vital for improving the quality of your breath and the energy circulating in your body.

Sitting in *Seiza*

Sitting in this posture allows energy to move up the spine and the heart centre to stay open.

1 Bend the legs slightly and place the right knee on the floor.

2 Next place the left knee on the floor with your big toes just touching. Your knees should be about 20 cm (8 in) from each other.

3 Bend forwards over your knees, then settle back to sit on your ankles. Your back should be straight, and your eyes should be relaxed, but focusing straight ahead of you.

Posture alternative

This posture is quite difficult for many Westerners to sustain for any length of time. If you feel muscle strain, place a cushion behind your knees.

Breathing exercise 2

The aim of this technique is to focus the mind on the *Hara* (see pages 104–105) and help to strengthen it. There is no point in practising these breathing exercises, or meditating, occasionally. You will not realize the benefits without having a regular routine, as the effects of any of the exercises change over time.

At first you may experience changes at the physical or emotional levels, followed by alterations in your perception of your energy. These will vary with each individual, so be aware that there is no set result that you should be looking for. However, these changes are the tip of the iceberg. It is only with regular practice that you will gain insight into what lies beneath the surface.

It may be difficult at first for you to visualize the energy expanding throughout the body. If this is the case, I suggest you place the intention in your mind that the energy will expand throughout your entire body, and that it is filling up the physical space around your body. The important thing is not to struggle with visualizing as this destroys the effect of the exercise.

As with the other exercises, build your practice up slowly, and if you experience dizziness take a break for 5–10 minutes, and then resume the exercise.

Before beginning, remember the principles of preparation (see page 60).

1 After placing your hands in the *Gasshô* position (see pages 62), put your hands on your knees with your palms facing upwards.

2 Begin with an out-breath, as in breathing exercise 1 (see pages 76–77). This will release stale air from the lungs. On the in-breath, breathe through the nose, bringing the breath down into the abdomen, and imagine it filling with energy. The abdomen will physically swell up, as in exercise 1.

3 On the out-breath, visualize the breath as energy that is expanding to fill your entire body, and leaving your body through your skin to fill the space around you. This requires you to pay less attention to the breath leaving the body via the nose and to put your focus on the *Hara* area, feeling it as the source of the energy leaving from it.

4 Finish by bringing your hands back into the *Gasshô* position.

Breathing exercise 3

This is a more advanced breathing technique. It is similar to some of the *Pranayama* techniques used in yoga, such as the alternate nostril breathing, as the aim of the exercise is to unite the right and left sides of the body to create a unified sense of self. It is also a very useful for developing the sensitivity in your hands that is so valuable when working with healing energy.

Begin by following the principles of preparation (see page 60). These help to settle you into the exercise and are a way of underlining the fact that you are entering a special space.

The Difficult Breath

People with respiratory problems are all too aware of their breathing.

When I was a teenager my father taught me yoga breathing techniques as a way of easing my asthma. As an adult my asthma eased off and after learning Chi Kung breathing methods, in which you control and extend the exhale, I began to see even more improvement. Combined with Reiki, these exercises will help to take the difficulty out of breathing for those with respiratory problems.

1 Sitting with the back upright, whether in the *Seiza* posture (see pages 78–79) or on a straight-backed chair or stool, place your hands in the *Gasshô* position (see pages 62–63) and hold them there. Take your mind down to your *Hara* (see pages 104–105) and keep your focus there.

2 On the in-breath, don't follow the path of the breath through the nose and down into the abdomen. Instead, as you breathe in, visualize energy coming in through your hands, flowing up your arms and down through the body into the *Hara*. With increased practice, you will feel, as well as visualize, the energy entering your hands.

3 On the out-breath, move the energy from the *Hara* back up through the body, along the arms and out of the hands.

Repeat the process, building up the number of repetitions gradually as with the other exercises. If you are experiencing problems with sensing the energy moving with the breath, don't agonize over whether or not you are doing it correctly – just trust that you are.

Hands-on or palm healing

We all use our hands to heal. When we touch someone to reassure them, or give them a hug, or kiss to make the pain go away, we are applying the comfort of touch, but we are also transmitting an energy to the other person that will help them to heal. Anyone who does energy work will be aware of this. However, those who are not involved in this work have perhaps only an inkling that there is something more powerful than just showing concern behind their instinct to touch a person or animal in distress.

Many people are aware that if they put their hands on their stomach when it hurts after a while it feels somewhat better. Their hands may get warmer, but they don't know why. This is not because they have a special talent – we can all transmit this energy to ourselves and others by placing our hands on the body.

The laying-on of hands, as it is sometimes called, for the purpose of healing, is a tradition in almost every society and culture. Some believe that healers are given a special gift from God. It is true that some spiritual and intuitive healers are able to draw sufficient energy for healing direct from the source without training in a practice such as Reiki. However, most people are using their own energy when they put their hands on themselves or another person to heal them. In the long run, this depletes their own store of *Ki*, and can lead to illness. This is why it is important to learn a practice such as Reiki.

Tap into fast-flowing energy

The hands-on healing of Reiki, or 'palm healing' as it translates from the Japanese word *Tenohira*, is by no means the only system of transmitting healing energy, but it is unique in the simplicity of learning the method. Compared with other practices, the Reiki energy is immediately accessed by the practitioner. Added to this, the energy flows fast and strong for most people from the moment of the first attunement (see pages 96–97), and can be accessed instantly the practitioner has the intention to use it. This makes it an ideal practice for the majority of people.

LEFT Often when we comfort someone by hugging them or touching them in some way, we are unknowingly using our hands to heal.

Traditional Reiki palm healing

Mikao Usui only added hands-on healing to his system of Reiki during the latter years of developing it. Now it is this aspect of Reiki that dominates the practice of the system. Palm healing was a very popular practice in Japan at the time Usui was establishing his Reiki system and, according to Bronwen and Frans Stiene in *The Japanese Art of Reiki*, one of Usui's students, Eguchi Toshihiro, was involved with some of the groups working with this form of healing. He later published a guide to hand positions for healing in 1930, just four years after Usui's death. It is now known that other students also published similar manuals.

When Usui started to teach palm healing, he taught it primarily as a form of first aid. Perhaps this reflects his own early experience with the energy, such as stopping the flow of blood from his toe when he came down from his mountain retreat. Information gleaned from his surviving students certainly suggests that he did not use a highly structured method of hand positions that treated the entire body, but may have focused on the head and on the parts that needed healing at the time. This reflects the fact that his early students were also advanced students of other esoteric practices, and thus did not require a structured technique.

The hand positions

It was when Usui started to teach more lay students that he saw the need for a more formalized approach, and asked his student Chujiro Hayashi to set out a series of hand positions that systematically worked around the body. It is likely that he asked Hayashi to undertake this task because of his medical training.

These hand positions may have been somewhat altered by Hawayo Takata, but this does not detract from the effectiveness of the system. Certainly, focusing the healing work on the chakras rather than the *Hara* during palm healing was only introduced in the 1980s, and is a purely Western interpretation of working with the system, although not one taught by Takata.

The hand positions do occasionally vary between the schools of Reiki but, as experienced practitioners know, the rules are simply a guide – the essence of the practice is in allowing the wisdom of the energy to guide your hands. (See Part 4 for a step-by-step guide to the hand positions.)

RIGHT Hands-on healing was a late addition to the Reiki system but now it is a dominant aspect of the practice.

Mantras

A mantra consists of words or sounds that are repeated as a form of meditation. Mantras are particularly associated with Eastern religious or spiritual practices. Perhaps one of the most famous mantras, known to many people whether religious or not, is *Om mane padme hum*, which is the principal mantra of Tibetan Buddhists.

Chanting a mantra is also the foundation of Transcendental Meditation, which is a very popular practice worldwide. Followers of Japanese Nichiren Shoshu Buddhism, another practice that has become popular in the West, chant the mantra *Nam myoho renge kyo* as part of their daily ritual. In Sufism, which is the mystical branch of Islam, followers chant *Allah-hu*.

It is the combination of the power of the word, the focus on the chant and the effect on the breathing that makes the mantra produce powerful transformations in the practitioner. With regular practice, it gives them spiritual insights and a sense of connection to the Universe.

Reiki has its own mantras. These are usually taught as being the names of the four symbols introduced at the Second and Third Degree levels. However, they are not strictly speaking names at all. In Japanese they are called *Jumon*, which

translates as 'sound which invokes a very specific cosmic vibration'. They are also called *Kotodama*, which means 'words carrying spirit'.

The Reiki mantras, which I abbreviate here to CKR (see pages 166–167), SHK (see pages 168–169), HSZSN (see pages 170–171) and DKM (see pages 190–191), come from a combination of Shinto and Buddhist origins. I have not written the mantras out in full, as anyone who has achieved the level of practice to use them will recognize them and be able to use them where they appear in exercises.

Chanting

If you wish to practise chanting the mantras, try the following procedure. Mantras are most effective when chanted aloud, so find a space where you won't be disturbed. Work with one mantra at a time for a period of 3–6 months so you become familiar with its unique vibration and effect. Repeat this exercise for as long as you feel comfortable, but be aware that it takes patience to build up a practice of chanting and feel the inner vibration.

Mantra exercise

The use of sound meditation is most effective when your body is upright.

1 Sit in the *Seiza* posture or upright on a chair.

2 Place the palms of your hands on your knees to keep you relaxed. Place hands in Gasshô if preferred.

3 Breathe in through the nose, drawing the breath down into the *Hara*. On the out-breath, speak the mantra clearly and correctly.

Japanese *Waka* poems

Japan may be better known now for exporting cars, games consoles and *Manga* (comics), but its poetry is one of its most enduring cultural exports. The tradition of writing poetry among the upper classes, along with the practice of calligraphy, has existed in Japan for centuries. Being of the Samurai class, Usui would have grown up with this tradition of writing poetry to express emotions, commemorate an event or record an observation of nature. His use of a particular style of poetry called *Waka* for meditative purposes was unknown until recently among Western Reiki practitioners but is becoming popular.

Usui used a selection of inspirational *Waka* written by the Meiji Emperor to help his students with their spiritual growth. All of these poems can be found in *The Spirit of Reiki* by Walter Lubeck, Frank Arjava Petter and William Rand. Opposite are two examples of *Waka* written by the Meiji Emperor, translated by Inamoto Hyakuten.

These *Waka* can be used as part of your meditation practice in place of the spiritual principles, or a *Waka* can be chanted like a mantra. Usui encouraged his students to chant or sing the *Waka* and become one with the insights they offer.

One suggestion for the development of your Reiki practice is to try writing your own *Waka*. Traditionally *Waka* had no concept of rhyme, or even of line, instead using units and phrases. The structure of the poem is typically five lines of 5, 7, 5, 7 and 7 syllables, although the example 'Sky' opposite is two lines, each of eight syllables.

Keeping a Reiki journal

For many years, I have encouraged students to keep a Reiki journal, particularly for the 21-day period after a class. Writing a daily journal is a form of meditation, and I would encourage everyone to take at least 15 minutes a day to release their thoughts and feelings onto a page. It is an invaluable way of clearing rubbish from the mind and allowing the creative soul to rise up and express itself. Although it is perfectly acceptable to use any type of notebook as your Reiki journal, you can honour your thoughts by taking the time to find one that pleases you visually, as you will feel more inspired to start writing.

Asamidori sumiwataritaru ohzorano, Hiroki onoga kokoro to mogana (Ten)
As a great sky in clear light green, I wish my heart would be as vast (Sky)

Akino yono tuskiwa mukashini kawarenedo
yoni nakihito no ooku narinuru (Tsuki)
While a moon on an autumnal night remains just the same as ever, in this world
the number of the deceased has become larger (Moon)

TRANSLATION, Inamoto Hyakuten

The universal use of symbols

Symbols have been used in all cultures since the earliest times and pre-date the written word. They possess a power that surpasses words, containing as they do a multitude of meanings that speak to the intellect, to the emotions and to the soul. Many of the symbols that still hold the most power for us today have their origins in ancient cultures, where they were used in art and religious ritual.

Often we cannot express what a particular symbol means, but we know that it speaks to us and it is something we feel in our hearts rather than in our minds. Symbols challenge us to go beyond the obvious and often the simplest have the most complex meanings.

Some symbols appear to be culturally specific, but, as with many religious beliefs, if we look at the broad canvas we will find that a symbol predominantly associated with one culture also appears in others, albeit in slightly different forms. The cross, which appears in various forms, is one example of this (see opposite).

The cross

The cross is predominantly associated with Christianity, and because of the global spread of this religion it is probably one of the most universally potent symbols. Other examples of crosses are the Celtic cross, a shape that brings together the cross and the circle. With its origins in an older earth religion, it represents the unity of male and female; the circle represents the female procreative energy and the cross the male energy. The Egyptian *ankh* represents the key to unlocking the mysteries of earth and heaven. As with the Celtic cross, the shape combines male and female energies. Both of these crosses pre-date the Christian cross.

The spiral

Another symbol that turns up across cultures, and is of particular interest to the Reiki practitioner is the spiral. Spirals and endless knots are especially evident in Celtic decoration. The spiral signifies the movement of energy, and the endless knot represents eternity. Similarly, in the yoga tradition, the *Kundalini* energy that leads to enlightenment is represented as a coiled serpent. This is effectively a spiral.

It is also believed that all energy flows in spirals, and that this represents the solar and lunar, male and female energies. This ancient concept of the spiral as representing the life force is reinforced by the discovery that human DNA is also a spiral.

LATIN CROSS · CELTIC CROSS · EGYPTIAN ANKH

PREHISTORIC SPIRAL

CELTIC KNOTWORK SPIRAL

Symbols in Reiki

The symbols used in Reiki that are taught from the Second Degree onwards have been a source of debate among the different schools of Reiki. The publication of *Essential Reiki* by Diane Stein in 1995 was a turning point in Western Reiki. Some teachers advised their students not to read it because it broke the rules. This point of view stemmed from the notions of secrecy and sacredness surrounding the symbols.

The traditional teachers teach the symbols following the method of Hawayo Takata. This entails the memorization of all the symbols during the class, and the disposal of all papers upon which the student has practised the symbols. In reality, this frequently means that students forget how to draw the more complicated symbols and are reluctant to ask their teachers to show them again for fear of being seen as less than perfect or lacking in dedication.

It is fair to say that at the point when the symbols were published there was an air of elitism within the Reiki community. It is my personal opinion that the debate forced the Reiki community to reflect on its attitudes, and that the symbols becoming public was inevitable due to a growing diversity in the forms of Reiki being taught, combined with rising use of the internet.

The four main symbols

Another issue regarding the symbols then came to light. It was discovered that when Hawayo Takata's Master students met after her death they found variations between the symbols she had taught them. If Takata did not teach the symbols uniformly, then it seems likely that many more variations have been passed on from teacher to student. There are now many additional symbols in circulation, but the majority of practitioners still focus on the main four.

After all this debate over the symbols in the 1990s, it was then discovered that Mikao Usui only introduced the four symbols late on in his teachings. Certainly it would seem that, unlike in the West, they were not the focus of his system. As with the formalized hand positions, he only introduced them as an aid to his students' practice. In Part 3 you will find more detailed discussion of each individual symbol, along with ways of meditating on them as part of your personal spiritual growth, and their use in healing.

RIGHT Mikao Usui introduced the four symbols only later on in his teachings, intending them to be used as a focus for meditation.

Attunements

In Western Reiki, the attunement is an integral part of any Reiki class. Teachers and schools may vary in the number of attunements they give at each level of Reiki, and in the method they use to pass the attunement, but nobody, as far as I know, teaches Reiki without this process of empowerment.

The story is rather different in Japanese Reiki. Mikao Usui gave a spiritual blessing, called a *Reiju*, to his students. This was not a one-time event, but was given frequently. The difference between a *Reiju* and a Western-style attunement is that the former is not intended to empower the person energetically in precisely the same way. It is almost certain that Usui was able to transfer or alter his students' energy without any formal ritual. However, when his students began to teach, they needed the support of a structured ritual, which probably led eventually to it becoming known as an attunement.

What is an attunement?

The simplest answer is that it is a form of spiritual empowerment that passes through the teacher to the student, which activates the ability to draw in more energy according to individual need, and enables them to become more effective channels for the Reiki energy. It is the individual aspect of the process that accounts for the fact that each person's experience is different. It is also an actual and symbolic means of initiating a person into a life with Reiki. It marks the moment between life without Reiki and a spiritual rebirth.

Each teacher will have different ways of conducting the initiation. Some may initiate several students at the same time in a simple, matter-of-fact way. Others will create elaborate sacred spaces and initiate one student at a time. In whatever manner it is carried out, it is a powerful experience for both the student and the teacher. Often when I am teaching a class I may start with no precise idea about when in the class I will carry out the attunement. I usually find that I am prompted by the Reiki energy itself, and at the right time I will suddenly feel myself, and the room, fill with energy at an extraordinary speed.

If you are new to Reiki you may be nervous about the process. Ask your teacher to explain by describing how they will move around you and what they want you to do, without detracting from the significance of the process.

LEFT An attunement is a method of spiritual empowerment that activates a person's ability to become an effective channel for the Reiki energy.

Energy and Body Systems

Eastern philosophies have detailed explanations of the movement of energy through the body, and of the workings of the energy body itself, that add to the Western concept of body systems.

The energy body

Reiki entails working with the energy body. What I am going to describe in this section is the energy body as it is understood in Chi Kung, as well as the chakra system – because the latter has become the prevalent energetic model in the West.

Working with the chakras was only added after Hawayo Takata died. Takata, Hayashi and Usui did not use this system; instead they focused on working with the *Hara* (see pages 104–105), which is integral to Japanese and Chinese energy work ranging from martial arts to Buddhist meditation.

The energy body is the one we cannot see, but which, through energy work, we can feel. It surrounds and penetrates every cell of our physical body, vibrating at a higher rate than it. Each person's physical body is unique to them, and has what might be called an energetic signature that is equivalent to the way in which fingerprints provide a unique personal identification.

I discovered Chi Kung some six years after finding Reiki. I was struck by the similarities between the energy I felt while doing Chi Kung exercises and giving Reiki. I mentioned this to my Chi Kung teacher. She agreed there must be similarities, so I asked her why she did not just practise Reiki as it was much simpler. She replied that, while I obviously liked the motorway, she preferred the scenic route. Certainly, much of what I learned through Chi Kung added a new dimension to my Reiki practice, and my understanding of the movement of energy, and the energy body itself.

The meridians, chakras and aura

Three elements of the energy body are relevant to Reiki: the meridians (see pages 102–103), the chakras (see pages 106–107) and the aura (see pages 122–125). The first two are different systems of understanding the mechanisms of the energy body, while the aura is common to both.

It is not crucial for the success of a Reiki treatment for the practitioner to have in-depth knowledge of all the meridians, or to know everything about the chakras. However, it does help to know the location of the physical organs.

Systems of the human body

In this section we will also look at two of the physical human body systems that are of primary importance in healing work: the endocrine system, which corresponds with the chakras, and the nervous system, which is our body's communications centre.

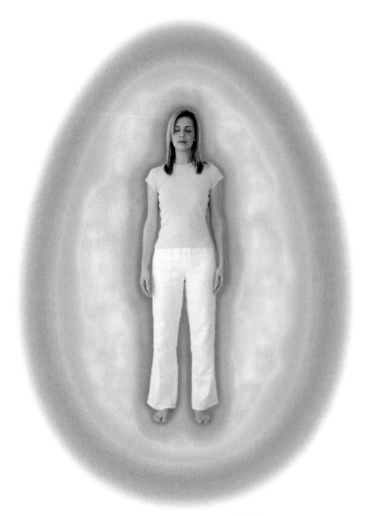

ABOVE The aura is an egg-shaped energy shield that surrounds our body and can expand and contract.

The meridians

In Traditional Chinese Medicine (TCM) the meridians are invisible energy channels that run in parallel with the physical anatomical system, but vibrate at a higher rate. Western science, as well as ancient Chinese and Indian scientific systems, suggests that energy vibrating at a higher rate has an effect on matter vibrating at a lower rate. We can deduce from this that if the meridians are adversely affected then the physical body will manifest the symptoms of ill health. The solution is to treat the energy body both by preventing imbalance and by rebalancing it.

There are 35 meridians in the TCM system, conducting Ki around the body. Within these there are 12 major meridians, 8 extra meridians and 15 collateral channels. It is along the major meridians and the Governor and Conception channels that all the main acupressure points are located. It is useful to know some of these as they can often provide some useful first aid (see pages 306–307).

The 12 major meridians are each related to a specific organ in the body. They are not 'connected' to the organ itself, but instead to the function of the organ. So, there are heart, lung and kidney meridians, and so on. Each meridian is also linked to the physical and emotional aspects of a person, and they are linked to elements. For example, the stomach meridian is connected with the element of earth, the colour yellow, sympathy, sweetness, flesh and dampness.

In TCM the flow of energy also follows natural cycles. We are well aware of the effects of the lunar cycle on the body, but less aware of the daily rhythm of the solar cycle. Energy is constantly flowing around your body and the flow of Ki peaks in each of the 12 major organs for two hours each day. For example, between 3 am and 5 am, the flow of Ki peaks in your lungs. If you have breathing difficulties you may find that during these hours you are awakened by them as a reaction to the increased energy.

Body part	Peak energy times
Heart	11 am – 1 pm
Gall bladder	11 pm – 1 am
Small intestine	1 pm – 3 pm
Liver	1 am – 3 am
Urinary bladder	3 pm – 5 pm
Lungs	3 am – 5 am
Kidneys	5 pm – 7 pm
Colon	5 am – 7 am
Pericardium	7 pm – 9 pm
Stomach	7 am – 9 am
Triple heater	9 pm –11 pm
Spleen	9 am – 11 am

The meridians

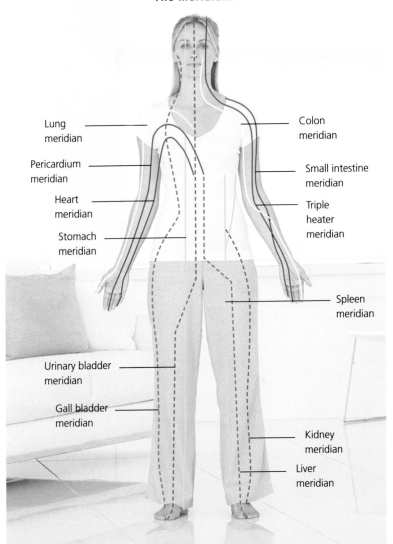

Lung meridian

Pericardium meridian

Heart meridian

Stomach meridian

Colon meridian

Small intestine meridian

Triple heater meridian

Spleen meridian

Urinary bladder meridian

Gall bladder meridian

Kidney meridian

Liver meridian

The microcosmic orbit and the *dantian*

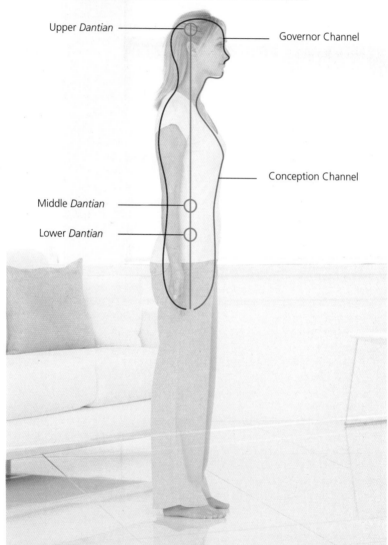

Upper *Dantian*

Governor Channel

Conception Channel

Middle *Dantian*

Lower *Dantian*

The microcosmic orbit and energy centres

Circulating *Ki* around the chakras in the body aids healing and increases awareness of the higher self. The two main channels or meridians on which the chakras lie are the Governor and Conception channels. The Governor (male/Yang) channel runs along the back from the perineum up the spine and over the head and the third eye to the roof of the mouth. The Conception (female/Yin) channel runs along the front from the tongue, through the heart chakra to the perineum. Together they create a circuit called the microcosmic orbit.

The *Dantian* and *Hara*

The focal point of the energy body in TCM consists of the three energy centres, referred to as the lower, middle and upper *Dantian*. These are linked to the Governor and Conception channels of the meridian system. The *Dantian* of most interest to both Chi Kung and Reiki practitioners is the lower one, which in Japanese is called the *Hara*. This is located just below your navel, and is the storehouse of your energy. This energy is not to be confused with *Ki*, but is the energy you were born with.

The middle *Dantian* is just above the navel and is the centre of emotions and of *Ki*, while the upper *Dantian* is concerned with our mental and spiritual aspects. It is

considered necessary in Chi Kung that you first learn to control the lower centre by grounding the energy there before you start working with the other two. If you don't learn how to ground energy first, then you may become physically and emotionally unbalanced.

The Three Treasures

At an even more basic level than the meridians and *Dantian* there are the Three Treasures, which are considered to be the foundation of our total composition. They are known as *Jing*, *Chi* and *Shen*.

- *Jing* is our inherited genetic energy which is associated with the lower *Dantian* or *Hara*. It is also our sexual energy, which needs to be preserved.
- *Chi* (*Ki*) is the vital essence we depend on for life. The quality of a person's *Chi* depends on the quality of their *Jing*. So, if we strengthen the *Hara*, which will allow us to tap into our *Jing*, we can improve the *Chi* flowing through us.
- *Shen* is our spirit or soul, which is fed by our *Chi*.

The system works upwards, with *Jing* feeding *Chi*, and *Chi* feeding *Shen*. We cannot change our *Jing* energy that we were born with, but by working with the *Hara* it can help us to support our *Chi*, which will improve our health and raise our spiritual consciousness.

The chakra system

Chakra is a Sanskrit word meaning 'wheel'. There are seven major chakras in the energy body, with the first situated at the perineum, or base of the spine, and the seventh at the crown of the head. The chakras are traditionally depicted as a lotus flower, which – when combined with the idea of a wheel – results in a circular shape spinning around its centre as the flower petals unfold. Each chakra has a number of attributes, including a colour, a relation to an element and the maintenance of specific physical and emotional functions.

Although most of us cannot see the chakras, it is possible to become familiar with how they are working by focusing our attention on their locations and concentrating on how the area feels. Apart from working with energy to influence the chakras, we can also work with colour and sound. For example, as each chakra is associated with a specific colour, you can meditate on drawing that colour into the chakra, or by wearing clothes of that colour to strengthen it. Some people also work with the sound vibration of each chakra.

Chakra	Colour of influence	Elements	Body sense
Base/Muladhara	Red	Earth	Smell
Sacral/Svadisthana	Orange	Water	Taste
Solar Plexus/Manipura	Yellow	Fire	Sight
Heart/Anahata	Green/Pink	Air	Touch
Throat/Vishuddha	Turquoise	Ether/Akasha	Hearing
Brow/Ajna	Deep blue	Spirit	ESP*
Crown/Sahasrara	Violet/gold	Spirit	All the senses

(*Extra-sensory perception)

The seven major chakras

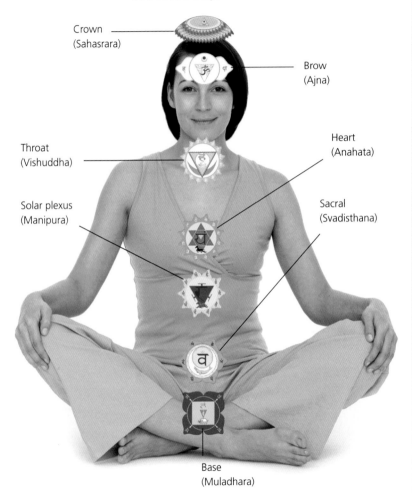

Crown
(Sahasrara)

Brow
(Ajna)

Throat
(Vishuddha)

Heart
(Anahata)

Solar plexus
(Manipura)

Sacral
(Svadisthana)

Base
(Muladhara)

Chakra 1

INDIAN NAME: **Muladhara**
WESTERN NAME: **Base/Root**

The base or root chakra is the first of the seven chakras. Situated at the perineum, between the anus and the genitals, this chakra opens downwards connecting the energy body with the earth. It is associated with security and mental stability as well as survival and prosperity.

There are numerous ways to work with this chakra to strengthen it, but at the centre of them all is the empowering decision to honour yourself whatever your circumstances, and make a point of connecting with nature and your own sexuality.

Chakra function

This chakra serves to ground us in the world. The earth energy is pulled upwards through the minor chakras on the soles of the feet, and up the legs, to balance this chakra. If you feel ungrounded, one solution is to take off your shoes and stand on grass or sand, which will help you absorb more earth energy. (See pages 152–153 for a visualization exercise that works on this chakra.) The energy is then pulled up the spine to balance the testes or ovaries, which are the parts of the endocrine system associated with the root chakra.

Physical health issues

Physical health problems associated with this chakra are ones affecting the feet, ankles and knees, as these are on the route through which the energy flows upwards. Other symptoms of being disconnected from the earth are lower back pain, particularly around the sacrum, which may leave you feeling physically 'unsupported', and problems with the sexual organs.

Mental and emotional issues

Giving us confidence in ourselves, and in the world, are two of the functions of the base chakra. The performance of this chakra throughout our life, if not worked on, is affected by our earliest experiences.

People who were born into a stable environment in which they felt protected will usually grow up feeling that it is safe to trust the world around them. They have little difficulty connecting with the earth energy and are open to receiving it. This keeps their base chakra functioning rather better than if they experienced trauma in the womb, or had an unstable childhood. People experiencing this kind of beginning in life will have a stressed chakra, which then manifests as a lack of trust in the world.

Chakra 2

INDIAN NAME: **Svadisthana**
WESTERN NAME: **Sacral**

 The sacral chakra is physically located just below the navel, in the same location as the *Hara*. The key element of the chakra is water and it is associated with our sexual energy. This refers to our life-sustaining energy rather than the energy we use for sex, which comes from the base chakra. The sacral chakra also has a strong association with the unconscious and with the creative impulse.

Chakra function

In both Hindu and Taoist teachings, the sexual energy associated with this centre may be transmuted to develop a higher spiritual consciousness by moving the energy up through the higher energy centres. It is these teachings that influenced the adoption of a celibate life as an expression of advanced spirituality. This of course is not something we all want to follow, and indeed an attempt to give up sex for the sake of spiritual advancement can result in psychosexual problems.

One of the main functions of the chakra is to help us form healthy emotional and sexual relationships. The energy may also manifest in the form of creativity, and it fuels our enthusiasm and joy in life. Dancing and singing are great activities to strengthen this chakra.

Physical health issues

Physical problems arising from the sacral chakra are connected to the adrenal glands. The adrenals govern how we react to stress. When we are confronted with a stressful situation, adrenalin is released to support our physical and mental ability to cope. However, if the stress is constant, we end up being unable to switch off the flow of adrenalin, and this damages our bodies.

The sacral chakra is governed by the element of water; therefore any dysfunction frequently manifests as a disease of the urinary tract and kidneys.

Mental and emotional issues

Dysfunction in this chakra often results in the inability to receive love. This can take the form of being unable to form relationships with the opposite sex. Sex itself may also be unfulfilling, as when the energy tries to rise through the chakras during lovemaking it may not be able to get past the blockages at the second chakra. Unblocked, this chakra enables us to experience unconditional love.

Chakra 3

INDIAN NAME: **Manipura**
WESTERN NAME: **Solar plexus**

 The solar plexus chakra is associated with the Sun (the *sol* in solar) and, therefore, connected with the element of fire. It is located at the level of the physical solar plexus, in the centre of the lower ribcage. It is usually associated with personal power, and is the place where we feel 'butterflies in the stomach' when we are in situations that affect our sense of power in both good and bad ways.

Chakra function

Think of this chakra as having the Sun in your body. It draws in solar energy, which then enables the flow of energy throughout the physical body. It could be described as an energy hub that feeds energy out along channels called *Nadis*, which are similar to meridians.

The last of the chakras before the central heart chakra, it is where we feel power, but also fear and anxiety.

Physical health issues

This chakra is primarily linked to digestion, but is more importantly associated with stress. The connection between digestive problems and stress is commonly seen in ulcers at one extreme, and in simple stomach upsets at the other. Of all the chakras, change in its functioning is perhaps easiest for us to sense because we have all felt the effects of stress in that area. Often what starts as an emotional feeling here quickly becomes physical. Diabetes is also associated with this chakra as it is linked to the pancreas.

One of the main ways in which you can strengthen this chakra is to look at stress-reduction techniques. Reiki, used regularly, is perfect for this, and you could add some more physical practices such as yoga or Chi Kung.

Mental and emotional issues

The solar plexus plays an important part in the perception other people have of us. The more energy we are able to draw through this chakra, the more attractive we will seem to other people, as we will be allowing our light to shine (not in an egotistical manner, but as a manifestation of natural self-esteem). Balance in this chakra also enables us to assimilate higher wisdom in our unconscious and access it for our healing.

On the negative side, dysfunction in this chakra tends to make us unhappy with life and appear arrogant.

Chakra 4

INDIAN NAME: **Anahata**
WESTERN NAME: **Heart**

 At the centre of the whole system lies the heart. Positioned in the centre of the chest, it is connected to the element of air and is the seat of the higher self. Universally thought of as the place where love originates, this chakra is associated with the qualities of passion and devotion.

Chakra function

The heart is associated with love and romance all over the world. This makes the organ itself an object of reverence. However, the heart chakra is not primarily concerned with romantic love, but with generating the energy of an all-encompassing love, such as the love of creation.

It is also the gateway between the three lower chakras that are more connected to the physical body, while the three above the heart are more associated with some finer emotions, our spirituality and higher consciousness.

Physical health issues

It is not surprising that this chakra is related to the circulatory system. Heart disease is probably the biggest killer of people in the West, but it is not just a disease created by an affluent lifestyle; it also has a stress component, in that feelings of frustration and anger are as bad for your heart as cholesterol.

We can go a long way to prevent physical heart disease by working to release the issues we hold in our heart chakra, such as emotional trauma, sadness and grief.

Mental and emotional issues

The highest form of love is unconditional love. Even romantic love can be transformed into this if we are able to form meaningful relationships that are respectful of another person's feelings. Perhaps we can only truly love another person in this way by first loving ourselves unconditionally.

Dysfunction of the heart chakra manifests as the inability emotionally to sustain lasting relationships or friendships. If we continue in this state, we eventually 'close down' our whole system, because we will neither give nor receive love.

To support your heart chakra, look for a therapy that will reduce stress and help you to release anger or acknowledge the sadness in your heart. Also, by giving yourself some self-love you will attract love from the Universe.

Chakra 5

INDIAN NAME: **Vishuddha**
WESTERN NAME: **Throat**

This chakra is associated with the element of ether and is located between the centre of the collarbone and the larynx. As this is also the location of our vocal cords, it is not surprising that this chakra is primarily associated with our outward communication, and the ways in which we express our inner self.

Chakra function

The throat chakra acts as a connection between the heart and the head. We often talk about acting from our hearts or our heads, and through the mediation of the throat chakra we express that action. In another sense, you could say it lies between body and spirit.

We can use our voice in many ways: to express love, to calm or to give praise. On the other hand, we can use it to express anger and negativity. When we use our voice in this way we create an imbalance in the chakra.

As a healer, you will often be able to hear if a person has an issue in this chakra just by listening to them talk. The words they use will obviously give you clues about their inner issues, but if you tune into the tonal quality of the voice, listening to it as if it was a musical instrument, you will gain much more insight into the person's character.

Physical health issues

Typically, physical ailments associated with dysfunction of this chakra are ear, nose, throat and respiratory problems. As the thyroid gland is also located in this area, hyperthyroidism and hypothyroidism are also indicative of imbalance.

When we have a deficiency in this chakra we become timid, fearful and afraid to speak up, whereas people with an excess of energy here are likely to be loud, and to talk excessively.

Mental and emotional issues

A blockage in this chakra may lead to closing down communications with other people. This in turn may lead to depression. People who find it difficult to express their inner feelings verbally may be helped by finding someone who will pay close attention to them, such as a counsellor who has been trained to listen in a non-judgemental way. The act of talking about problems will help to remove any blocks.

Chakra 6

INDIAN NAME: **Ajna**
WESTERN NAME: **Brow/Third eye**

 The brow or third eye chakra is located in the centre of the forehead, just above the eyebrows, and like the throat chakra is coupled with the element ether. It is the chakra associated with the mind, and particularly with intuition and psychic abilities. It is also the chakra we are drawing on when we meditate.

Chakra function

The mind is the least-understood aspect of the human being. The mind is not simply the brain, as it is so much more than the sum of that organ's parts. This chakra enables us to move beyond the mind as we experience it every day with its constant chatter and movement of thoughts, and tap into the knowledge and wisdom we have within, but of which we are unaware.

Dysfunction in this chakra can lead us to become arrogant about having special powers of insight, or psychic abilities, and use them to control other people.

Physical health issues

Physical problems associated with this chakra are ones that affect the head in general, and the eyes. Therefore, headaches and migraines are symptoms of imbalances in this chakra. These can be relieved by strengthening this chakra through quiet meditation to calm the mind and release tension.

Also, most of us constantly overstress our eyes by working long hours in front of a computer screen. This is another major cause of headaches, and you should try to take your eyes away from the screen as frequently as you can, and if possible look at a plant or gaze out of the window at the sky. The colours of nature and the energy of natural matter are healing in themselves.

Mental and emotional issues

In comparison with the other chakras, the brow chakra is not really linked with emotions as such. However, an imbalance here can strongly affect the pineal gland, which sits in the centre of the brain, directly behind the eyes.

This gland is responsible for the production of serotonin and melanin, hormones that affect our mood and our sleep patterns respectively. The pineal gland is light-sensitive; therefore, a lack of light reduces the amount of serotonin released, resulting in seasonal affective disorder (SAD), which often manifests as a depressive state.

Chakra 7
INDIAN NAME: **Sahasrara**
WESTERN NAME: **Crown**

The ultimate chakra is directly opposite the base chakra and is located on the crown of the head. Whereas the base chakra faces down towards the earth, the crown chakra opens upwards towards the heavens. It is not associated with any element, and it is the chakra that must not be closed at any time, meaning that healers should be very careful when working around this area.

Chakra function
Just as the base chakra connects us to the earth we live on, the crown chakra connects us to everything that transcends our earthbound state. It is the chakra that keeps us connected to a universal consciousness, and through it we can experience the state of pure being, and of transcendental consciousness.

Physical health issues
As with the brow chakra, dysfunction in the crown chakra can lead to headaches, particularly ones caused by the denial of particular feelings. A tendency to be obsessive is also a mark of imbalance here.

Epilepsy is another symptom associated with the chakra. Healers working with people suffering from epilepsy should ensure that the person is also receiving medical treatment.

Mental and emotional issues
Denial of life, obsession and the bottling up of anger – also linked to the heart chakra – are connected with the crown. These emotions can result in a physical illness such as high blood pressure, which is associated with the emotion of anger. A degenerative disease, such as Parkinson's, is also linked to dysfunction in this chakra – the symptomatic shaking may indicate a fear of life, and if we become paralyzed we are denying life completely, for we are unable to move.

The Thousand-petalled Lotus
The name Sahasrara means 'a thousand petals'. The lotus flower is used as a symbol for all the chakras because the flower itself grows up from the mud and rises through the water to blossom fully in the light. This reflects the human condition of being temporarily earthbound and our physical bodies being composed of earth elements. The water represents our emotions, which we have to work through until we reach the spiritual light represented by the Sun.

Case study: chakras

A friend asked me to give him a Reiki treatment as he had heard good things about it and wanted to try it out. He practised an earth religion and was familiar with energy work. He always appeared outgoing and confident and had a very pleasant speaking voice. After I had finished the treatment, I told him I had felt an imbalance in the throat area and suggested that he wore something turquoise or silver near to the throat chakra.

He told me that he felt very nervous about speaking in front of other students on the postgraduate course he had just started. This seemed surprising, given his personality, but confirmed what I had felt. After several weeks he returned to tell me that he had been wearing a blue stone around his neck, and now had no problem with speaking in class.

The endocrine system and chakras

The function of the endocrine system is to secrete chemicals called hormones throughout the body via the bloodstream, and in doing so to regulate the action of the organs and tissues.

Malfunction of the endocrine system leads to problems suggesting imbalance such as diabetes, hyper-thyroidism and infertility, all of which are caused by hormone levels that are either too high or too low.

The glands that comprise the endocrine system are:
• The pituitary
• The pineal
• The thyroid and parathyroids
• The thymus
• The islets of Langerhans in the pancreas
• The adrenals
• The gonads (testes and ovaries)

The main gland of the endocrine system is the **pituitary**, which is located in the brain along with the **pineal** gland. The pituitary coordinates all the other glands and also produces the hormones that influence growth.

The **thyroid** gland, in the neck, controls our metabolism. The **parathyroids**, which are attached to the thyroid, are essential for the maintenance of healthy bones,

nerves and muscles, and also balance calcium and phosphorus in the body.

The **thymus**, which is situated near the heart, keeps our immune system healthy.

The **islets of Langerhans in the pancreas** are responsible for the secretion of insulin and glucogen to maintain correct levels of glucose in the blood. When insufficient insulin is produced, glucose levels rise, resulting in diabetes.

The **adrenals** lie above the kidneys and produce two types of hormones. The outer layer is the source of steroid hormones that balance the salt, sugar and water concentration in the body, while the inner layer supplies adrenalin necessary for stimulating our 'fight-or-flight' reaction to stressful situations.

The **gonads** (testes and ovaries) secrete the hormones necessary for reproduction. Women with an imbalance of hormone secretion in the ovaries manifest symptoms varying from infertility to irregular menstruation and pre-menstrual syndrome (PMS).

Familiarize yourself

As you will see from the diagram on page 119, this system has correspondences with the chakra system. People engaged in energy work should make themselves familiar with the endocrine system in order to understand various conditions.

The human endocrine system

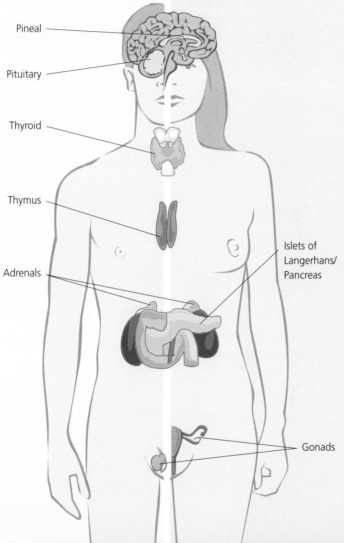

Pineal

Pituitary

Thyroid

Thymus

Adrenals

Islets of
Langerhans/
Pancreas

Gonads

Each of the seven chakras corresponds to one or more of the main endocrine glands (see pages 114–115).

The base chakra

Linked to the ovaries in women and the testes in men. The ovaries produce the hormones oestrogen and progesterone. Oestrogen is associated with the menstrual cycle, while progesterone is needed to prepare the uterus to receive the fertilized egg. The hormone in the testes is testosterone, which promotes male characteristics and sperm production.

The sacral chakra

Connected to the adrenal glands that sit above the kidneys and produce adrenalin and cortisol. Adrenalin primes our body to react to stress by raising both the heart rate and blood pressure. Cortisol is our natural anti-inflammatory, and cortisone-based treatments are common in Western medicine for symptoms that include inflammation, such as those associated with arthritis.

The solar plexus chakra

Associated with the Islets of Langerhans, which produce insulin to lower blood-sugar levels and glucogens to raise them. Diabetes and hypoglycaemia stem from malfunctions in this gland.

The heart chakra

Closely linked to the thymus gland, which is the control centre of our immune system, and operates our defence against viral-type infections and airborne germs, such as flu and colds.

The throat chakra

Linked to the thyroid gland, which produces thyroxine and iodothyronine. These promote human growth and are responsible for cell repair. Thyroid problems are a result of either a lack or an excess of these hormones.

The brow chakra

Associated with both the pineal and pituitary glands. The pineal gland secretes both serotonin and melatonin, which are responsible for maintaining mood and sleep patterns. The pineal gland in particular is light-sensitive and is similar in structure to the retina of the eye.

The crown chakra

Like the brow chakra, associated with both the pineal and pituitary glands. The pituitary gland coordinates all the other glands in the system and as such secretes a number of hormones. Obviously, any problems with this gland will have a knock-on effect throughout the whole endocrine system.

The endocrine glands and the chakras

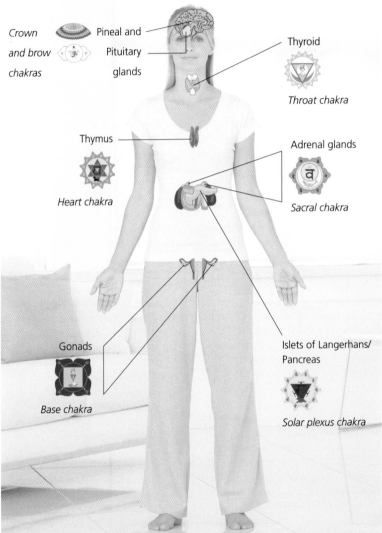

Crown and brow chakras

Pineal and Pituitary glands

Thyroid

Throat chakra

Thymus

Heart chakra

Adrenal glands

Sacral chakra

Gonads

Base chakra

Islets of Langerhans/ Pancreas

Solar plexus chakra

The nervous system

While the endocrine system orchestrates the hormones, the nervous system is the body's control and communications centre. The central nervous system is situated in the brain and spinal cord and controls our conscious and unconscious functions. The peripheral nervous system, consisting of sensory and motor nerves, sends messages to this central system.

The common problems associated with the nervous system are those associated with the brain area, such as stroke or cerebral haemorrhage. Migraine is another problem, as is meningitis. Psychological problems such as depression, anxiety and insomnia are also associated with the nervous system and may be caused by chemical imbalances in the brain.

The autonomic nervous system

All the systems in our body are interconnected so that the body works harmoniously. The system that demonstrates this connection and interdependence, and is of particular interest to energy workers, is the autonomic nervous system. This includes part of the peripheral and central nervous system and controls functions that occur without conscious effort.

Most importantly, the autonomic nervous system is composed of two parts:

the sympathetic and parasympathetic. These are responsible for regulating heartbeat, blood pressure, breathing rate and body temperature, among other things. Parts of the system also respond to emotional stress. The sympathetic system deals with involuntary body functions such as breathing. It also activates the adrenal glands in response to stress. Conversely, the parasympathetic system is most active when the body is in a relaxed state, and it also helps the body recover from a stressful episode.

These two systems need to be in balance to maintain good health. If the sympathetic system is constantly overused, as is often the case in modern living which imposes increasing amounts of stress, it works against our efforts to maintain balance. If we fail to use the parasympathetic system to return to a state of relaxation, it becomes weakened, and (as with unused muscle) it takes time to return to full function. Regular meditation, yoga, Chi Kung and Reiki are all excellent ways of balancing this important body system.

The human nervous system

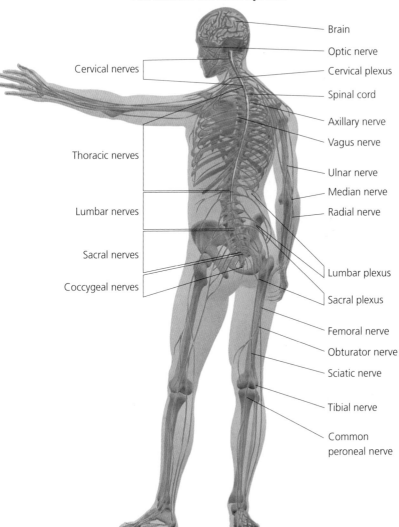

- Brain
- Optic nerve
- Cervical plexus
- Spinal cord
- Axillary nerve
- Vagus nerve
- Ulnar nerve
- Median nerve
- Radial nerve
- Lumbar plexus
- Sacral plexus
- Femoral nerve
- Obturator nerve
- Sciatic nerve
- Tibial nerve
- Common peroneal nerve

Cervical nerves

Thoracic nerves

Lumbar nerves

Sacral nerves

Coccygeal nerves

The aura

The final element of the energy body, and the one common to both the meridian and chakra systems, is the aura. The aura is an egg-shaped field of energy that completely surrounds the human body, even extending beneath the feet. It is sometimes described as a 'rainbow of light' as it contains all the colours of the rainbow, as do the chakras (see page 106). The purpose of this energy field is to support the growth of the physical body, and in this respect it is like an energy grid that exists before the body does. In other words, it may form at the time of conception, although it cannot be detected after death.

Echoing the number of colours in a rainbow, the aura also has seven layers

Layer	Colour	Aspect of energy body	Quality
1	Red	Etheric body	The five senses
2	Orange	Emotional body	All emotions
3	Yellow	Mental body	Intellectual activity
4	Green	Higher mental body	Interaction with other people, plants, animals; relationships of all kinds
5	Blue	Spiritual body	Connection to the divine
6	Indigo	Causal body	Experience of the spirit world
7	Violet	Ketheric body	Connection to our higher self and our superconsciousness

(see page 101). The first layer of energy, closest to the body, has the densest vibrations; these grow successively lighter and faster as the layers get further away from the body. The first layer is red, which is also the colour of the base chakra. The second layer is orange, corresponding with the second chakra – and so on, with the final layer being the violet associated with the crown chakra. Each of the layers is connected to an aspect of the energy body, as shown in the table (opposite).

Seeing the aura

The aura can be perceived by some people, and clearly many cultures have been aware of its existence for some time, as energy fields around the body and is represented in the visual art of a number of civilizations. In the West, the halo is the most common depiction, and is symbolic of the spiritual character of the person.

People who can see auras may have been born with this gift, but it can also be developed. Those who can see them say that everyone's aura is constantly changing, depending on mood, health and level of spiritual development. The size of a person's aura also changes. It can expand to fill a room and touch all the other auras present, or it can be pulled in close to the body like a protective shield.

This expansion and contraction of the aura means that we can pick up information from the auras of people around us. You may be inexplicably drawn to someone, for example. This probably indicates that there is something in their aura that you resonate with. Similarly, your aura may contract if you sense something you don't like.

BELOW The aura has long been depicted in religious art, often as a halo, indicating that its existence has been recognized for some time.

Practising sensing the aura

There are three simple ways to practise seeing auras. In all of these methods you need to let your eye muscles relax, so that while you are looking directly at the person or plant you are not pulling the eyes into focus with the muscles. Don't expect to see the energy of the aura clearly at first, but relax and allow yourself to get the sense of a shimmer around whatever you are looking at.

Method 1 Sit outdoors and gaze at a plant or a tree that is silhouetted against a plain backdrop, such as a clear sky. Trees have very strong energy fields.

Method 2 Hold your own hand up against the sky and spread your fingers wide. Look between the fingers and around the outline of your hand.

Method 3 Ask a friend to sit or stand against a white wall. Keep the light dim and observe what you can see around the body.

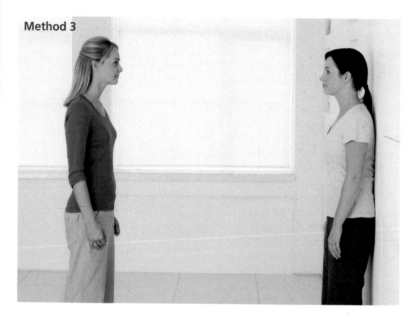
Method 3

Cleansing your aura

You may want to use a smudge stick and feather to cleanse your aura and the healing space (it is easier if someone else can do this for you).

1 Light your smudge stick and have a fireproof bowl filled with sand or earth at hand to extinguish it.

2 Moving the smudge stick around the body, use the feather to disperse the smoke through the aura. This removes any harmful elements in the aura.

Living with Reiki

Reiki heals every aspect of our lives. It is a practice that cures our ills, soothes our emotions and enables us to create the life that we want.

Reasons to practise Reiki

Everyone follows their own path to working with Reiki. The yearning of the soul for something more may lead to an encounter with Reiki in which the inner self says 'this is what I need'. Perhaps a person will only journey with Reiki for a brief time, yet the beauty of the practice is that it will always be with them, and they will always be able to return to it.

There are many reasons to practise Reiki, the most common one being the desire to heal others, while others will choose it because it is a holistic system for healing oneself. Both are valid reasons. It seems selfish to want to heal ourselves first when we should be doing good for the rest of the world. Of course, we have it the wrong way round when we think like this. It is ourselves we must heal before we can help anyone else.

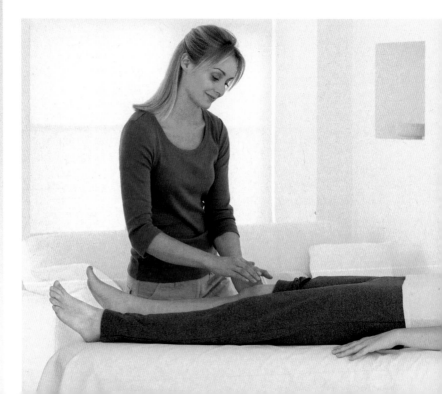

Benefits of Reiki

Regardless of the motivation each person has for wanting Reiki in their life – and each individual's reasons are right for them and not to be judged or compared with others – there are many benefits that come with the practice. First of all, these will be felt on a physical and emotional level. Reiki supports the body's ability to heal itself by restoring its energy balance. It strengthens the immune system so that all types of illnesses can be resisted, or at least overcome more quickly. It can also be used as a treatment for a number of conditions (see Part 8) and it is one of the most effective reducers of stress that can be used by the individual without having to seek treatment elsewhere. It can also be used with other therapies (see Part 9).

Once we feel better physically, we are often more able to turn our attention to the less tangible issues we face. On an emotional level, it promotes a sense of being at peace with oneself, and can also, sometimes painfully, reveal the root cause of our feelings and behaviour. Yet Reiki, no matter how challenging the cleansing process, always teaches us that nothing ever stays the same. What seems like despair today can be transformed into relief tomorrow as we release the emotional baggage that has been weighing us down.

Reiki also offers us the opportunity for spiritual development. It is much more than a therapy – it is a multi-faceted practice that when used on a daily basis feeds the soul.

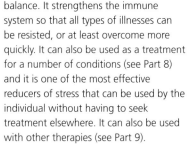

LEFT The yearning of our soul for something more may lead us to an encounter with Reiki in which we recognize it as that 'something'.

Reiki and you

The only person responsible for your life is you. However, given the way most of us have been socialized, accepting this is more difficult than it sounds for many people. We are not encouraged to take responsibility for our lives; instead we are socialized to do what other people want us to do. If we don't follow this 'norm', we are led to believe that we will not reap the benefits society has to offer us, and if we really don't 'play the game' we will be banished to its outer fringes until we come to our senses.

From birth we are taught to conform to other people's wishes rather than our own. Parents, teachers and even friends impose their belief systems on us, mostly with the best intentions, and also because they know no different way to guide us. As a result, it is challenging for us to have any clarity about who we are and what we believe. To find yourself among all this cultural conditioning requires a step back and some introspection.

This does not mean removing yourself from the everyday world, although many have made that choice throughout history in seeking the solace of a monastic life. To stay in the world, and find our inner truth, we need an aid that will provide us with the tools to make our way through life in a way that balances our body, mind and spirit.

Religions have sought to be that aid, and have provided it to a large extent for a great number of people. However, that which contented our ancestors is not always sufficient today. The hunger to go beyond the teachings of orthodox religions is apparent even among those who follow them. This has led to many people looking at the more esoteric aspects of the major world religions and integrating them in their lives.

Reiki for all

Reiki is one of the tools we can use to guide us through life. Its simplicity makes it accessible to everyone and its lack of dogma means that it can be practised by everyone, regardless of religious beliefs. Reiki promotes physical health, mental clarity and spiritual advancement, and can be incorporated into any lifestyle. You don't have to go anywhere special to practise it – Reiki is available everywhere you are, and you are never separate from it.

RIGHT Reiki enables us to take responsibility for our own life and empower ourselves. Moreover, its healing power is available at all times, and in all places.

Reiki in your daily life

It would be a daring person who attempted to practise yoga or Chi Kung while travelling on a train to work. However, a Reiki practitioner can always give themselves Reiki wherever they are, and nobody will notice. Sitting quietly, with your hands on your legs, or perhaps folded across your stomach, you can use the daily commute to work as an opportunity to give yourself healing. You can use it in the same unobtrusive way at work to boost flagging energy levels, or to calm yourself in a stressful situation. You can even send Reiki to conflict in the office. This is just one of the benefits of making Reiki a part of your daily life.

Flexibility

The system is so flexible, with numerous ways to incorporate it into your lifestyle, that you will always be able to find an approach that suits you. There are no rules telling you that you 'must' do this or that. Instead, you are in charge. You may want to include meditations and chanting alongside giving self-healing, but you decide when and where. There is nothing forced upon you in Reiki. You take responsibility for your practice and develop it at your own pace.

Added to this, Reiki can be applied to an astonishing number of facets of your life. You can give Reiki to all your family members, including your pets, as illustrated in the chapters that follow. You can give Reiki to your food, whether you are in a restaurant or eating at home. This will lift the vibrations of the food and improve its nutritional value. You can also give your house Reiki treatments, and even your household appliances such as a washing machine or computer. Everyone and everything around you can be included in your practice.

You are the centre

It is important to remember to keep yourself at the centre of your practice. Strengthening yourself will change the way in which you experience the world. Family relationships will improve or resolve themselves for the good of everyone. Problems will melt away as your perspective on them changes. You now have a tool to work with, so that when you are faced with a challenge, no matter how mundane, you will have the confidence to trust that the outcome is perfect for your life.

RIGHT Reiki is a flexible system, which puts you at the centre, and which you can develop at your own pace.

The energy shower

The exercise that follows is one of my favourite from Chi Kung, but it can be used by Reiki practitioners to boost and cleanse their energy levels in just a few minutes every day. In Chi Kung it is called 'Shower of Light' and it is a wonderful way to cleanse your body with energy, after you have cleansed it with water. Reiki practitioners simply need to have the intention for the Reiki energy to flow through the hands while doing the exercise.

1

1 Stand with your spine straight, shoulders down and body relaxed. With your arms at your sides, turn your palms to face outwards and upwards. Breathing in, slowly start to raise your arms on both sides.

2 Continue raising your arms until they are above your head. Keep your arms loose and rounded in shape at all times. (It is better if you can complete steps 1 and 2 while inhaling only. However, if you cannot do this at first, it is better to exhale when you need to, rather than hold your breath.)

2

3 **4**

5

3 When your arms are above your head, feel the connection to the Reiki energy through your palms, and imagine more energy pouring into your palms from the sky.

4 As you exhale, slowly bring your hands, palms facing inwards, down over the top of your head, in front of your face and down the front of your body until they reach your navel.

5 Visualize the energy cleansing away any harmful energy, and repeat the whole sequence 4–6 times.

Reiki and Western medicine

Reiki essentially complements Western medicine, meaning that it acts with it to help conventional treatments. It is not the case that anyone has to choose one or the other. Be careful as a Reiki practitioner never to suggest that Reiki is a substitute for medical treatment, no matter what your personal beliefs are.

You should also never attempt to make a medical diagnosis. Even though I believe it is important for a Reiki practitioner to have basic medical knowledge, as well as some familiarity with anatomy and physiology, we are not qualified to tell another person that they may have a condition, even if it seems apparent they may do. If a practitioner suspects a client has an undiagnosed condition, he or she must find a way to suggest the client sees a qualified physician without causing alarm.

Specific conditions and medication

Similarly, if a person comes to you for treatment of a specific physical condition, I suggest you find out if they are having medical treatment, and if they are not it is advisable to suggest they do see a doctor. Although Reiki practitioners have never been required to take down detailed medical histories from their clients in the same way as other therapists, it is a very

good idea to have some discussion, especially about chronic conditions such as diabetes, as Reiki could affect the levels of insulin needed after the treatment.

If they are on medication, establish what it is and do some research on it so that you are aware of the way the drug works and its possible side-effects. However, at no time should you discuss the appropriateness of the treatment or advise them to alter their dosage. There are plenty of good guides to medicines available, and if you are treating people regularly you should make yourself familiar with the drugs popularly prescribed for common conditions.

Working with hospitals

In the last few years, Reiki has made its way into hospitals in a number of countries, and some doctors are aware of the benefits it can bring to patients with chronic conditions and terminal illnesses, as well as those recovering after an operation. It is wonderful to see all types of healers being given salaried jobs in health services. However, as these are still limited, Reiki practitioners can always work on a voluntary basis.

RIGHT Although Reiki practitioners do not make a medical diagnosis, it is sensible to take down a client's basic medical history.

PART 3
The Three Degrees of Reiki

The First Degree

Taking the first step on your journey with
Reiki opens up a new world of healing
experiences that range from healing yourself
and others to healing your home and
healing the world.

Choosing a Reiki Master

In most cases, people make their choice of a Reiki Master based on the recommendation of friends. This is a fairly reliable way of doing it, although it must be remembered that the needs and beliefs of friends are not the same as your own. Many people find their teacher through some synchronicity that leads them to the right person at the right time. As with other spiritual paths, experiencing this type of 'coincidence', where you have the right encounter just when you need it, happens all the time with Reiki.

My own experience of finding a Reiki Master had a strong element of synchronicity. A friend lent me a book about Reiki that she had just received from her sister in India. It was *Empowerment through Reiki* by Paula Horan, and was one of the first books available about Reiki. I read it and knew immediately that I wanted to learn this practice. However, neither I nor my friend knew where we could find a teacher locally. I felt sure I would find a teacher, even though none of the alternative directories listed any.

Two weeks later I was passing my local pharmacy, which had a natural remedies section. A magazine in the window caught my eye so I bought a copy and in the classified advertisements found a Reiki Master offering treatments and classes.

I immediately had a treatment with her. I didn't go on to take the First Degree with her as she had certain beliefs I didn't feel comfortable with but my search for a teacher continued and through a series of phone calls to various organizations I eventually found my first teacher.

Do your homework

If you are looking for a Reiki teacher, it is important to consider the many differences of approach to the Reiki system that exist, and decide which one is for you by doing some research. It is also important to talk to the teacher before taking their class. A teacher you feel compatible with, and whom you feel you can trust and respect, will always be better for you than one you feel uncomfortable with. The journey you are about to embark on with this teacher is one where you need to feel safe, and there is no reason to choose a teacher you mistrust just because somebody else tells you they are the best around. The best teacher for you as an individual exists, and you will find them – or, as the saying goes, 'the teacher will find the student'.

RIGHT When choosing a Reiki teacher it is important that you feel comfortable with them and that their beliefs are compatible with yours.

Healing experiences and responses

A person's experience of a Reiki treatment and the way they respond is unique to them. So, if you are new to giving treatments to other people, don't expect to see a uniform response, and don't expect your experience of channelling the energy to be the same every time either.

One early experience of my own with the variations in energy came when my teacher asked for volunteers to help her give Reiki at an exhibition. I was working with an experienced practitioner when a man approached the stand and asked for a treatment. When I put my hands on his shoulders to connect with the energy, I remember thinking it had a different shape to any I had experienced before. When I visualized the energy I could see jagged peaks, whereas when I had visualized the energy in other people it always seemed to be like rounded waves. I talked to the other practitioner about it afterwards. She asked me if this was the first man I had given Reiki to, and I replied it was. Her opinion was that I was seeing very strong male energy that was in stark contrast to the female energy I was used to.

Not everyone will experience the difference between male and female energy in the same way. This was my experience, and an early one in my practice, but it was certainly useful in teaching me that I could expect to find differences between people, and between treatments.

Some people seem to absorb and flow with the energy during a treatment, whereas with others you may feel resistance and struggle. Some people have dramatic visual experiences, while others may experience strong physical sensations. Some simply see changing colours, and others have no recollection of what they experienced. Whatever the experience, you can be sure that the person is receiving healing – perhaps not in the way they expect, and possibly not in the way you expect, because even though we should have no expectations about the process we very often do.

Expectations limit healing. When we are young we learn by using our logical mind: if you touch something hot it will burn you, so once experienced we avoid repeating it. When it comes to healing we cannot apply the same logic. Suppose you are treating a specific condition and you observe a particular response. The temptation of logic is to look for a similar response the next time you treat the same condition. However, healing is unique to the individual and requires us to keep our minds open.

RIGHT When you give Reiki to someone, it is best to have no expectations about how they will respond.

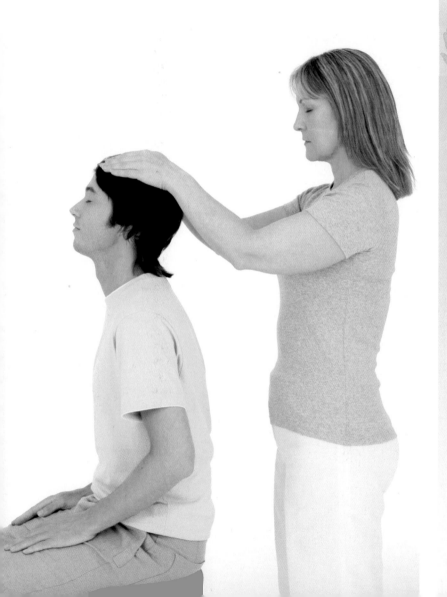

ABOVE Rose's story illustrates the dramatic healing experienced by some recipients.

Case study: Rose's story

With some people there is an immediate and dramatic healing experience that often feels like a revelation. Rose's story is an example.

Rose was a woman in her 60s with a grown family. She had largely brought them up alone, her husband having left her. She was visiting her daughter, who had a beauty salon, and where I had a treatment room. One day I asked if she would like to try a treatment. She knew nothing about Reiki, but with encouragement from her daughter she agreed to give it a go. She explained to me that she had a hip problem that was due to be operated on.

When I reached the back of her heart chakra, I sensed a sudden change in energy. As I kept my hands there, I felt someone behind me put their arms around me and place their hands over mine. In that moment I felt absolutely sure that these hands over mine belonged to Jesus. Suddenly there was a very strong sensation of release in the energy, and I felt guided to move my hands on.

As I reached the final hand positions, with one hand on the hip and the other on the sole of the foot, Rose's hip seemed to dissolve under my hands and I had the sensation of my hand going right through her body. At the end of the treatment, we didn't discuss what had happened and Rose went for a rest.

An hour or so later, Rose's daughter came to tell me what her mother had experienced. When my hands had been on the back of her heart chakra, she had experienced complete forgiveness towards her husband who had deserted her. All the anger and bitterness she felt left her in that moment.

She returned home and set about finding a Reiki class. Furthermore, her hip no longer gave her the same problems. In only one treatment Rose transformed her life and drew on, in my opinion, the true heart of her Catholic beliefs to receive the healing energy of Jesus.

This is an example of the way in which each individual draws to them exactly what they need from Reiki, and the way in which it works with other belief systems.

Using the First Degree

The first level of Reiki can be used in so many ways. The only thing that is missing from this level is the ability to send distance healing, which is learned at the second level. Therefore, many people find that the First Degree is sufficient in itself. First Degree Reiki can be used for:

- self-healing
- healing others
- healing animals and plants
- bringing energy to your environment
- energizing food and drink.

Self-treatment

Self-healing is the most important first step in Reiki, because without healing yourself you cannot heal others. Giving yourself Reiki every day is an essential part of this. I always ask students to give themselves a full self-treatment every day for the first 21 days after their First Degree class. Of course, I would like it if they continued with daily self-treatments after this period, but I realize that not everyone has time for a full treatment every day. The 21-day period after any class is the most important for clearing old energy and bringing yourself into balance.

The hand positions for self-treatment are shown in Part 4. Each position should be held for approximately 3–5 minutes, but if you need to hold a position for longer follow your intuition. If you don't have time for a full treatment every day, a little Reiki is better than none. The more you give yourself Reiki, the more familiar and at ease you will become with the energy and the length of time you need to hold each position.

Make yourself comfortable when giving yourself a treatment. Your bed or the sofa are the best options. Some people like to give themselves a treatment before getting out of bed; others prefer last thing before going to sleep. It all depends on what suits you. Although if you do choose last thing at night it is unlikely you will get through a full treatment before falling asleep.

The effects of self-treatment are cumulative. The more regular your practice, the more benefits you will feel. There may be times when you don't want to bother giving yourself Reiki. This is normal, but if this attitude persists please take a moment to consider what is behind it. Perhaps you are feeling that you don't deserve time for yourself, or maybe you are letting life dictate a pace that you would rather not have, but which you can see no way out of. Whatever the reason is, don't feel guilty about it – just acknowledge it and resume your practice.

RIGHT Self-treatments can both energize and heal you. They also help you to understand energy better.

Inanimate objects and personal problems

Two aspects of working with the First Degree which are perhaps less discussed than the others are working with inanimate objects and with personal problems. The latter get more attention in the Second Degree, but there are ways to work with them at the first level.

Reiki for inanimate objects

People tend to laugh if you mention the idea of giving Reiki to your computer or fridge. But it does work, and it is not that odd if you think back to the explanation of the nature of energy in Part 1. Everything originates from the same energy, including the materials used to make a washing machine. They just vibrate at a different rate to animal matter.

If one of your household objects breaks down, put your hands on it and let the Reiki flow. Try not to give it Reiki from an attitude of anger about it having broken; instead send the energy with gratitude for the service it has given you. You should also give the Reiki without expectation of a particular outcome. You may still need to repair or replace an item, but there is healing somewhere in the situation.

Reiki for personal problems

At a meeting after my First Degree class, one of my fellow students told us that she had been trying to sell her house for months but was having no luck. Now she had several potential buyers after going around her house giving Reiki to the walls.

The Reiki teacher told us that even at First Degree level we could give Reiki to issues we were troubled by. One way to do this is to write the problem on a piece of paper, hold the paper between your hands and give Reiki to the situation. Be clear and positive in your statement. For example, always write 'I want' rather than 'I don't want'. You must also be open. If you want a new relationship, don't specify the person you want a relationship with. At the end of my 'wish', I always add these words: 'This or something better now manifests for me in a totally satisfying and harmonious way for the good of all concerned.'

LEFT When you give Reiki to an object, send the energy to it with gratitude for the service it has given you.

RIGHT Write a problem on a piece of paper and send Reiki to the situation with intentions for it to be healed.

Grounding your energy

As an energy worker, it is important to know how to ground your energy, and if you are teaching others or giving treatments you should be able to show others how to do it. You should also be able to recognize when others need to be grounded.

One of the symptoms of being ungrounded is a 'spaced out' or dizzy feeling. It can also manifest as a sensation of coming out of the body. This is caused by not being sufficiently connected to earth energy. One way to ground is to stand on grass or earth in bare feet as often as possible (see pages 108–109). However, after giving a Reiki treatment, or after receiving an attunement, that may not be sufficient.

Visualization exercise

I use the following exercise for grounding and I also teach it in Reiki classes. Read the instructions through several times. Alternatively, get a friend to read them to you for your first few attempts, or record them, so that you can listen to the instructions. Please don't worry if you cannot 'see' everything as described.

1 Find a straight-backed chair or a stool that allows you sit with your feet flat on the ground. Remove your shoes, but if it is cold keep your socks on.

2 Close your eyes and breathe deeply three times. Visualize a rope descending from the tail of your spine, through the floor, into the earth, through layers of rock, until you feel you are at the centre of the earth. Anchor your rope there.

3 Now imagine that there are two holes in the soles of your feet and a heavy, brownish-red sludge is coming up through these holes and circulating throughout your lower body as far up as your waist. Let this energy circulate until your body feels heavier.

4 Next visualize a distant point in the heavens from which a beam of white light is coming down to connect with a point on the crown of your head. Feel this light flow through this point in your head and through the upper part of your body, cleansing it and making it feel lighter.

5 Now feel the two different energies circulating at the same time. Finish by touching the floor with your hands and allowing any excess energy to return to the earth.

Healing your home with Reiki

It was not until I had taken the Second Degree that I really awoke to the possibilities of using Reiki in the house. I had been using it on inanimate objects such as my watch and my computer, but I could not really see a way to use Reiki to fill my environment, apart from the techniques suggested at the First Degree level, which did not quite help me achieve what I had envisaged.

I read books on sacred space and space-clearing techniques, and once I had taken the Second Degree I created ways to combine some of these with use of the Reiki symbols as part of my housework routine, to great effect. However, the more I worked with the energy, the more I realized that my perception that I didn't need to have the Second Degree before I could clean the energy of my home, and that I could have been doing it effectively with the First Degree.

RIGHT Salt is used for purification in many cultures. Use it to purify your home as well as your own aura.
BELOW To heal a room draw Reiki symbols in the centre and corners, or visualize your home filling with Reiki.

After cleaning the house physically, you can now clean it energetically. To do this, go round each room and draw the CKR symbol (see pages 166–167) in each corner of the room. You can, if you wish, also draw the symbol in the centre of the room and visualize the entire space filling up with Reiki. You can also go round each room with a smudge stick, again paying attention to the corners of the room where energy tends to get stuck. This is a similar technique to cleaning the aura with a smudge stick (see pages 124–125).

If you have not taken the Second Degree, simply use intention and visualization to fill your home with Reiki. You can hold your palm up into the corners of the room and imagine the energy flowing from your hand and cleaning the area.

Using sea salt

Another practice that can aid energy cleaning is throwing pure sea salt into the corners of the room, again after you have cleaned first. The salt needs to be swept up later and thrown out. If you watch Japanese Sumo wrestling, you will notice that the wrestlers throw salt into the combat space, the intent being to cleanse the area and remove any negative vibrations from previous matches. Salt is well known for its cleansing qualities. When added to your bath, for example, it helps to cleanse your aura and ground you, as well as healing open wounds.

Healing the world with Reiki

There is always trouble somewhere in the world. War and famine claim the lives of thousands daily, and those of us who don't directly experience either of these during our lifetime are sadly a statistical minority among the world's population. Nevertheless, even those of us not directly affected live in a climate of fear. Daily messages are pumped out by the various media about the threat of terrorism, economic recession and environmental disaster. The damage to the environment is the only one that we feel we can have some control over by making individual efforts to stop the desecration of the planet.

Yet we can make a positive contribution to the resolution of all the issues the world faces by sending healing energy to them, whatever level of Reiki we are practising. If you have taken the First Degree, you can use the same method as with personal issues. Write the situation on a piece of paper and hold it in your hands. Visualize the situation and have the intention for the healing to flow there and produce a solution for the highest good. Again, don't ask for a particular outcome, as that may not be for the greatest benefit. While it may seem contrary to logic that loss of lives is a benefit, we cannot second-guess the Universe. We can only help by sending energy to support the best possible outcome. If you have the Second Degree, you can use the CKR symbol (see pages 166–167) to intensify the energy, along with the HSZSN symbol (see pages 170–171), which will add another dimension to the healing.

Another solution is to form a group with other Reiki practitioners and regularly send Reiki to global and local situations. Groups of light workers or energy workers meet regularly all over the planet to send healing, and have been doing so for many years. We can all be a part of this energetic network that supports the world with love.

The Great Invocation

Although the invocation opposite is not strictly a part of Reiki, it expresses a wonderful sentiment that is worth contemplating when we want to heal the world with energy. The version of the prayer reproduced here was channelled by the esoteric writer Alice Bailey in the 1940s. Although it refers to Christ, it uses the title as representing all the spiritual Masters – therefore it does not belong to any one religion.

RIGHT By gathering together in groups and sending Reiki to world situations we can play a part in resolving conflict and support the world with love.

From the point of Light within the mind of God
Let Light stream forth into human minds
Let Light descend on Earth.

From the point of Love within the heart of God
Let Love stream forth into human hearts
May Christ return to Earth.

From the centre where the Will of God is known
Let purpose guide human wills
The purpose which the Masters know and serve.

From the centre which we call the human race
Let the plan of Love and Light work out
And may it seal the door where evil dwells.

Let Light and Love and Power restore the Plan on Earth.

Version by Alice Bailey

The Second Degree

The desire to advance your Reiki practice brings you more deeply in touch with the mysteries of energy and the ways in which it transcends our ideas of Time and Space.

Developing your practice

The desire to advance and have more knowledge is a natural one. Reiki is taught over three levels, but the decision as to how far to advance, and when, is one to be taken by both the student and teacher.

The decision to progress from the First to the Second Degree ideally reflects a commitment on the part of the student to become more deeply involved with Reiki, and in changing their life. In other words, it should be a conscious decision rather than an automatic one, as the attunement takes people through processes that are deeply connected with their mental and emotional being, and they enter into a cleansing process on this level. This may not always be a pleasant experience. The teacher also needs to be capable of supporting students who find that long-buried hurt and anger is emerging and overwhelming them. This deep cleansing is of great benefit in the long term, but students should be prepared for it, and guided in working through it. This is one of the reasons for having time gaps between Degrees, although many teachers don't observe this convention now. In my opinion, however, there are benefits in taking your time.

Take your time

Many teachers, however, do have rules about when you can progress to the Second and Third Degrees. For example, when I first discovered Reiki back in 1992, the teachers of the Usui Shiki Ryoho insisted on a three-month minimum period between the First and Second Degrees. Now it has become fairly common to do both in one weekend, although I should add that this does not apply to all schools of Reiki.

Although I work as what is called an 'independent' Reiki teacher, I believe there is good reason to follow some of the more orthodox rules and have this minimum period. First, it allows time to adjust to the new energy, and to appreciate the changes. Second, it gives time to gain more understanding and insight into how the energy works before going deeper into the process.

We live in a fast culture and our expectations are geared towards quick results. When we consider the years of training that Mikao Usui went through to arrive at the creation of the Reiki system, it should make us reflect on our need for the instant fix, and consider allowing our Reiki practice to deepen slowly but surely.

RIGHT In a world of fast fixes, it may be more fruitful to develop your Reiki practice at a slower pace.

The significance of the symbols

In Part 2, the universal use of symbols as well as aspects of the debate among Reiki schools over the Reiki symbols were discussed (see page 94). In this section I will look at each of the symbols and the ways of using and meditating on them.

The symbols were not part of Mikao Usui's initial Reiki system. According to Japanese sources, he only introduced the symbols when he started teaching Reiki to people who did not follow any spiritual practice. In other words, as aids to spiritual development. They were to act as a focus for the mind, in a way that is similar to the use of mantras. Usui's symbols combine both a visual and aural focus, although in the Western tradition there is more emphasis on the visual aspect.

Teachers of the various schools will have different opinions about the significance of the symbols. The main teaching is that the symbols increase the power of the Reiki that a person is channelling. A view closer to Mikao Usui's intent when he introduced the symbols is that they have no power of their own but act as a focus for our intention.

Using the symbols

What is required is that we connect to each symbol and the aspect of the Reiki energy it manifests. When combined with an inner understanding of the vibration of its accompanying mantra, we can dispense with the symbols altogether and simply focus on manifesting the energy connected with each one. This is by no means simple and it may take a practitioner many years of meditating on each symbol before this can be achieved.

There are four main symbols that are taught by the majority of schools. There are also many new symbols around, which have been channelled by the founders of some of the newer Reiki systems. The focus here is on the symbols traditionally associated with Reiki, the characteristics of each symbol and the aspects of the Reiki energy they are intended to manifest.

Secrecy of the symbols

As discussed on page 94, there is a notion of secrecy surrounding the symbols and mantras so they have not been published in this book. Anyone who has been taught Level 2 will know the symbols and mantras and be able to follow the instructions for their use on the following pages.

RIGHT The symbols act as a focus for the mind and, thus, are an aid to spiritual development.

Sensing the symbols' energy

This exercise will help you to work with the symbols in a meditative way. If you feel dizzy afterwards, you must ground your energy. You can use the exercise on pages 152–153, or any other technique that works for you. You might also consider doing this meditation for shorter periods if you are becoming ungrounded by it.

Usually the symbols are drawn using the whole hand with the palm facing outwards. Some people prefer to use the index finger, or the index and middle fingers together to sign them in the air. You can also visualize them being drawn without having to make any hand movements, or trace them on the roof of your mouth with your tongue. These last two techniques are obviously useful when you want to use the symbols but don't want anyone to observe you doing so, perhaps simply because you are in a public place.

Finally, you may also want to visualize the symbols as having colour while meditating on them. The colour may appear spontaneously, and it would be interesting to keep a journal (see page 90) where you can observe the relationship between changes in colour and the qualities of the energy.

1

1 Sit in a meditative posture and breathe down into your *Hara* until you feel your body relax completely.

2 Raise your right hand, keeping the palm flat and facing away from you. Draw the symbol in the air, and repeat the mantra for the symbol out loud three times. Visualize the symbol where you have drawn it, or in your mind's eye. Continue repeating the mantra on the out-breath. Practise this for 5–10 minutes, gradually building up the length of time you are able to focus.

Symbol 1 – CKR

The form of the first symbol, at least in part, can be found in cultures outside Japan. A student of mine once took me to a famous cathedral in England, dating from the Middle Ages, to show me her discovery of this symbol in parts of the interior stonework. The symbol can also be seen in the Hindu and Celtic cultures.

The characteristic of the energy associated with the symbol is Power in the Western schools, and Focus in the Japanese teachings. Please remember that what we think of as the name of the symbol is actually the mantra associated with it, which when repeated will manifest the same vibration as the visual symbol. This symbol has no name. It is a pure symbol, and should simply be referred to as Symbol 1.

In the Japanese teachings that influenced Usui, this symbol is also associated with Earth energy, which we need to be grounded. This is also the energy found in the *Hara*, which is unique to you from the point of your conception. It is your connection to the universal life force. Connecting with this symbol by meditating on it will help you to increase this energy.

This first symbol is perhaps the most widely used and versatile of the three symbols taught at the Second Degree level. This is due to the fact that it acts to focus the Reiki energy on whatever it is directed at in a way that intensifies the energy. Its action could be compared to training a bright light on something, or using the precision of a laser.

You can visualize the symbol as being of any size. For example, I visualize it covering my entire home for protection, especially when I am going away.

The symbol can be used independently, as can all the others. Some teaching suggests that it is necessary to use this symbol to activate the others, but this is not the case. It can, of course, be used in combination with the others.

The mantra – CKR

When you use the mantra in conjunction with the symbol, always repeat it three times. It is not necessary to know the literal meaning of the mantra because the power is in the vibration of the sound it makes when spoken aloud. Indeed, the need to know the meaning is a mental distraction. However, for the sake of being able to answer questions about its meaning, translations of the mantra vary from 'increase the power' to 'spirit that comes directly from the supreme existence'.

RIGHT The first symbol connects us to the universal life force through Earth energy, and the energy in the *Hara*.

Symbol 2 – SHK

Like Symbol 1, this is another pure symbol. It is associated with emotional and mental well-being in the Western teachings, and with Harmony in the Japanese tradition. Both these describe it well, as it brings peace of mind and emotional balance.

In contrast with Symbol 1, the second symbol draws on the energy of Heaven, which may also be referred to as Light. Using this energy helps us to develop our intuitive and psychic abilities, reflecting its association with the mind. It also connects us to the energy of the higher self or spirit.

It is beneficial to draw and visualize this symbol when you want more mental clarity about a situation. It is drawn on the brow chakra both in self-healing and when treating others, as is traditionally taught. When sending distance healing, it is useful to focus more on this symbol when the person receiving the healing seems to be in mental or emotional distress.

The energy of this symbol is rather subtle and may be more difficult to discern than that of the other two symbols taught at the second level. For this reason, it may not get given as much attention by students. However, persevering with this symbol brings its own reward according to what you need at the time. It can be used along with Symbol 1 if you wish to enhance the process of emotional cleansing.

The mantra – SHK

As stated before, when using the mantra with the symbol, repeat it three times. If you wish to work with the mantra alone, you can chant it repeatedly as described on pages 88–89.

Translations of the mantra vary from 'I have the key' to 'mental habit' to 'the earth and sky come together'.

It is important to say the mantras accurately, just as it is important to draw the symbols as precisely as possible, according to the form you were taught. Accuracy is not required for its own sake, but because it reflects a mindfulness about what you are doing. Drawing a symbol or chanting a mantra has little or no effect if you do it while having your mind on other things. The energy is in the intention and the energy will go where your mind leads it.

LEFT The second symbol is associated with the energy of Heaven/Light and connects us to our higher self.

Symbol 3 – HSZSN

Symbol 3 is not a symbol in the same sense as Symbols 1 and 2 because it is actually formed from five Japanese *Kanji* that can be read as a sentence. It is this sentence which forms the mantra of the symbol.

The characteristic of the symbol in Western Reiki is that of sending energy across a distance, and in the Japanese system it is simply thought of as Connection. These are not so dissimilar, as when we send healing energy through time and space we are truly connecting with the Universe and each other. If we look at it like this, we are not sending healing as though we were separate from the person we are hoping to help; instead we are becoming One with them so that they can heal themselves.

Indeed, when working with this symbol on other people, you may have the sensation of becoming part of the other person. You may feel as though you are inside their body or mind, and are experiencing the world as they are. This ends as soon as the treatment is finished. It is very important when using this symbol to clear the connection when you have finished, just as you would clear your aura at the end of a physical treatment.

The wonder of this symbol is that it connects you not only with people over distance, but also with yourself at any time in the past, present or future, enabling you to heal aspects of your life that you maybe thought you could do nothing about. For example, many people experience remarkable healing of relationships with parents who have died, removing feelings of guilt and anger and allowing them to move forwards freely in their lives.

The mantra – HSZSN

Even though this mantra is formed from actual *Kanji*, there are still a number of translations. Unlike in the Roman alphabet, each *Kanji* has several meanings, so establishing a uniform translation into another language is almost impossible.

Some translations are 'I am correct consciousness', meaning that in a state of correct consciousness we achieve Oneness. Other more New Age translations are 'no past, no present, no future' and 'I unite with God'.

RIGHT Symbol 3 embodies the ability we have to send healing energy through time and space, becoming One with other people wherever they are.

Reiki and ritual

Ritual has many meanings. It can mean something done routinely, but which has some special significance for the person who is doing it, or it can be a ceremony only experienced at certain times in life. Either way, ritual is connected with the quality of marking a time or event.

You might have a cup of tea or coffee every morning when you wake. This is your ritual for marking the beginning of the day. You might pray every night before you go to sleep as a way of drawing a line under the day. Every major religion is built around a variety of rituals, the three common to all being the rituals of birth, marriage and death. Ritual, whether mundane or spiritual, gives structure to our lives.

Reiki has a number of ritualistic components that help us to structure our practice. For example, the hand positions for treatments, while flexible, provide us with just such a ritual structure to observe on a daily basis. Meditations on the mantras and symbols are another element that you can choose to develop into a personal ritual.

LEFT Ritual in every form, whether spiritual or mundane, brings structure to our lives and is often a way of celebrating special events.

Attunement ritual

Perhaps the most important ritual associated with Reiki is that of passing an attunement (see also pages 96–97). This has the quality of defining a singular moment of change in the life of a student. I cannot think of another spiritual practice that has an equivalent act that engenders such profound change in such a brief time.

Ritual surrounding the attunement process varies from teacher to teacher. Some enjoy preparing a sacred space with incense, flowers, candles and pictures of Mikao Usui, Chujiro Hyashi and Hawayo Takata, while others may keep it simple and free of New Age or religious symbolism. Each student will undoubtedly find the teacher with the style that suits them best. The decoration of the space matters less than the intention with which the teacher approaches the ritual of passing the attunement.

The attunement ritual appears to have come from Tendai Buddhism. Mikao Usui may not have used the physical movements most teachers will be familiar with, owing to the fact that he was able to conduct the process energetically. However, most of us need the physical ritual to support the energetic process of opening the space around and within the student for the Reiki energy to enter.

Distance healing

One of the many reasons people want to progress to the second level of Reiki is the prospect of being able to give distance healing treatments. These days, family and friends are frequently scattered all over the world, and when they are ill, or facing a problem, it is wonderful to be able to offer them help when it is not possible to physically be with them. Indeed, many of my students reveal their wish to help a parent who is about to have an operation, or who has a chronic condition, as one of their reasons for learning the technique.

At the second level you will be taught how to use Symbol 3 (HSZSN) to connect with the person who wants healing, and the use of Symbol 1 (CKR) to intensify it. It is important to remember to say the mantra of each symbol when using it, repeating it three times. Giving a distance healing is simple, although you will need to find a place where you will be undisturbed for 20–30 minutes.

Asking permission

Before giving a distance healing, the first thing you need to remember is the ethics involved in it. It is important that you have the permission of the person to give a treatment. Sending Reiki without the other person's consent is like rushing up to someone and placing your hands with the intent of giving them Reiki without asking them first. If it is an emergency and you cannot ask them, visualize them, draw Symbol 3 over the visualization and ask them at the level of spirit if they want to receive it. You will be able to sense their response. If it appears to be negative, stop the treatment and see them surrounded by blue healing light to protect them. At all times respect their choice without judgement.

Timing

If possible, arrange a time for the healing session so that the person receiving the treatment can also find a place to relax and tune into the energy. This will increase the benefits of the treatment for them, whereas if you do it while they are engaged in another activity they won't be able to focus on themselves. It could also be dangerous, as the energy may make them feel drowsy, so driving a car or operating machinery while receiving a treatment is not advisable.

How to carry out distance healing

Four main methods of giving a distance healing are taught. Each method is extremely easy to use from a practical point of view, and you need little equipment to carry them out. Although it is easier to send healing from a quiet space the methods may also be easily used discreetly in public.

Method 1 Write the person's name on a piece of paper and draw the symbols over it, again enclosing the paper within your hands.

Method 2 Draw the symbols over your left hand and visualize the person being held in your hand. Then cover them with your right hand to enclose them.

Method 3 Draw the symbols on a photograph of the person, enclosing the photograph within your hands.

Method 4 Use a substitute to represent the person; draw the symbols and use the hand positions on the object.

My own preference is to use a photograph when possible, as this helps me to focus better than the other methods. When a photograph is not available, I use the visualization technique.

During the treatment it is vital that you don't impose your own 'need' for the person to be healed on the session. The treatment is most effective when you allow the Reiki to flow while you stay neutral and let the person take what they need from it, just as with a physical treatment.

You can either visualize working through all the hand positions of a standard treatment, or simply visualize the person drawing the Reiki into their whole body. Experiment with different methods until you find the way that enables you to focus best.

Finish off the treatment by smoothing off the person's aura in your mind and drawing Symbol 1 (CKR) over them. I then disconnect by blowing between my hands three times. An alternative is to clap your hands three times. Follow this with your usual routine for finishing a treatment and cleansing your aura.

My own distance-healing experiences

I must admit that initially I was a little sceptical about the power of distance healing to deliver as effective a treatment as a hands-on one. It was not until I experienced it myself that I appreciated its potency.

I had contracted chicken pox from my son and was giving myself treatments several times a day, which had certainly alleviated the worst of the symptoms. However, I felt very weak and I was behind with organizing a workshop for a Reiki teacher from India. He phoned to ask how it was going and I explained the situation. He said he would send Reiki for the next three days. That night I felt an intense burning around my kidneys. The second and third nights were the same, but on the morning of the fourth day I woke up to find all my symptoms had disappeared. I felt as though I had never been ill.

This increased my confidence in using it with other people, and in response the Universe sent people to me who wanted healing for their friends and family.

Case study: the musician

The son of a student of mine was assaulted and received a fairly serious head injury. Although this had healed, he was depressed and afraid to go out. His mother asked me to give him treatments with his permission.

My immediate impression of him during the first treatment was of somebody submerged under water. This impression continued over the next few treatments, with a feeling of anger also emerging. Then one day I 'saw' him get out of bed and sit at a desk. He was writing a composition on music manuscript paper. I knew nothing about his personal interests, but I felt this activity was key to him healing.

I called his mother and asked her if he had any interest in music. She told me that he was top of his music class at school for both composition and playing, but that he had not bothered with it since the attack. Being a Reiki practitioner and an artist, she understood that encouraging him to focus on his musical talent would lift his depression and give him confidence again. It also provided him with a reason to get out of bed that came from his soul. Reiki provided this much-needed insight, showing the many ways in which healing occurs.

Preparing a space to treat others

Before treating other people, you need to prepare yourself energetically and prepare your work space. The latter particularly applies if you are operating a professional Reiki practice.

Ideally, you should use a massage table for giving treatments. You can use a bed or a quilt on the floor, but only if you are giving treatments infrequently, otherwise you will end up with back problems. If you are using a table, cover it with a sheet or the paper covers used by massage therapists. You will also need a light blanket to cover the client, as the

body becomes cold quickly when relaxed. Also make sure you have a box of tissues near by, as a treatment can be a very emotional experience for some people.

Create a relaxed atmosphere

If you are working from home, choose the room that you feel will be most relaxing for giving treatments. In an ideal world, you would have a room in the house that can be used for Reiki alone – as this is impossible for many people, select the room that needs the least work to switch it from its everyday function to a room for Reiki. The most important thing, whatever the circumstances, is that the room is clean, quiet, warm and comfortable.

Air the room well before the treatment and burn some incense before the treatment rather than during it. Some people, especially those with bronchial problems, are irritated by incense as it tends to give the air a dry quality. Alternatively, you can scent the room with an oil burner, choosing a light oil such as lavender that promotes relaxation. You might also want to clean the room energetically using the methods described on pages 154–55.

LEFT It is advisable to burn incense before the treatment begins as some people are irritated by it. Burning oil is a better solution.

ABOVE A treatment room should be clean, comfortable, quiet and have been prepared with care and respect.

Another thing to consider is noise. While it can be pleasant to work with a window open, too many sounds from outside can become a distraction for the client. Similarly, put any telephones on 'silent' and use an answering machine.

One sound that does complement a treatment is that of music. However, keep the volume at a level where the music can be heard by the client but is not obtrusive. Each practitioner will have their own musical preferences, but I like to choose something that is without lyrics, and is melodic, relaxing and non-energizing and will, therefore, not disturb the client.

Preparing yourself to treat others

One of the first priorities before giving a treatment is to pay attention to your personal hygiene. Your clothes should be clean, your hands washed and your teeth brushed. This ensures that no offensive smells, such as those of garlic or tobacco, get in the way of the client's comfort. You should also remove your watch and any jewellery that might get in the way, especially bracelets and rings, although you may keep a wedding ring on if you wish. When I wash my hands just before beginning the treatment, I like to put a tiny drop of rose essential oil on my hands.

The next step is to cleanse yourself energetically. The method that follows is from Chi Kung, but it is remarkably similar to the recently discovered technique used by Japanese Reiki practitioners for removing toxic energy.

Meridian massage

The intention of this exercise is to cleanse blocked and negative *Ki*. The exercise requires at least six repetitions of the steps, eventually building up to 36. Once you have mastered the technique, you will build up a flowing rhythm that will make this number of repetitions easy to complete. It is not necessary to do this before every single treatment if you are giving several in a day. At the beginning and end of multiple sessions will be sufficient.

1 In a standing position, place your left hand on your right shoulder and raise your right arm.

2 Stroke down the outside of your right arm as you swing the arm down and across your body.

3 When your left hand reaches the fingertips, your right hand then strokes up the inside of your left arm to the shoulder as you bring your left arm above your head.

4 When your right hand reaches your left shoulder, sweep it down the outside of your left arm to the fingertips, swinging the arm down at the same time. Now the left hand strokes up the inside of the right arm to the shoulder, which is the position you started at.

1

2

3

4

Medical conditions and Reiki

As mentioned previously, Reiki can be used with any condition. Unlike certain other therapists, the Reiki practitioner is not expected to take a medical history, as they will not be manipulating the body physically or introducing any elements, such as oils, that a person might have a reaction to. However, although one of the chief benefits of Reiki is that the energy acts only for the good of the receiver, there are times when caution is needed.

Broken bones

Don't treat the site of a broken bone before it has been set, as there is a chance that the energy will start to knit the bone at an incorrect angle. This could result in it having to be rebroken. By all means give the person Reiki for shock (see pages 308–309), but keep your hands away from the break itself. Once the bone has been set and plastered, give as much Reiki as possible to the site of the break.

Severed body parts

Reiki accelerates healing, so any accident where a part of the body, such as a finger, has been severed also requires caution, as the tissues and nerve endings need to be reconnected surgically. Giving Reiki directly to the wound area may cause it to start closing up before surgery can be performed, causing problems for a successful reattachment. Again, treat the person for shock and pain, focusing your attention on the heart chakra.

Pacemakers

I was taught to check if a person has a pacemaker fitted. The reason given for this is that the effect of Reiki on such a device is unpredictable. While I very much believe that Reiki does no harm, I recognize the logic behind this advice because a pacemaker works with electrical currents and an energy surge could affect the rhythm. Should you encounter this issue, discuss it with your Reiki teacher and with the client.

Diabetes

I was also taught to be cautious with diabetes, because Reiki may affect the levels of insulin in the body. Therefore you should advise any recipient with diabetes to monitor their insulin levels closely after a treatment and alter their dosage accordingly. Since I was taught this, treatment of diabetes has changed enormously and it is much easier now for people to monitor levels and adjust dosages according to their needs.

RIGHT Although it is the nature of Reiki to never cause harm to the receiver, it is advisable to be aware that some conditions require caution.

The Third Degree

Following a call to teach Reiki to others is
a vocation and requires a commitment to
guiding others on their spiritual journey and
helping them to realize their full potential.

Becoming a Reiki Master

The Third Degree trains the student to become a Reiki Master and teacher. There are differences in approach to this training between the traditionalist schools and the newer independent ones. Essentially, becoming a Reiki Master is about wanting to assist others to realize their potential. Each person must examine their own needs and beliefs and choose the training and teacher that are right for them.

Traditionalist approach

Within the traditional schools, such as the Usui Shiki Ryoho, Masters will only take on a limited number of students at this level, usually preferring to teach one student at a time. This is not necessarily an elitist approach. Instead, it is based on the idea that anyone wanting to become a teacher should have a deep understanding of Reiki accumulated through a regular practice, and a high level of commitment to it.

There are good reasons for this. A teacher needs to have a mature and responsible attitude to developing a spiritual practice and to taking responsibility for their life in general, as they will be guiding others through a process in which they will also be expected to achieve the same level of maturity and responsibility. Therefore, students must be able to demonstrate their aptitude for this to their Reiki Master.

Students will therefore be expected to have been practising Reiki for some time and it is up to the individual Reiki Master to evaluate each student individually. They will accept the student if they think they are ready and, more importantly, if they are convinced that this is the right step for the student.

The training usually takes place over a period of a year, during which time the student will assist the Master at First and Second Degree classes, and with other tasks such as organizing Reiki share groups and doing administrative work for the classes. It is very similar to an apprenticeship, and they will also be taught how to teach.

Independent approach

The approach of independent teachers differs from that of traditionalists in three ways: (1) they tend not to be as stringent in their selection of students; (2) the training may last as little as one day; (3) the costs are significantly lower. The argument for this approach is that the higher costs of traditionalist training effectively exclude a lot of people who would be excellent teachers and healers.

RIGHT People wishing to become Reiki Masters ideally have a commitment to healing and a strong desire to help others achieve their potential.

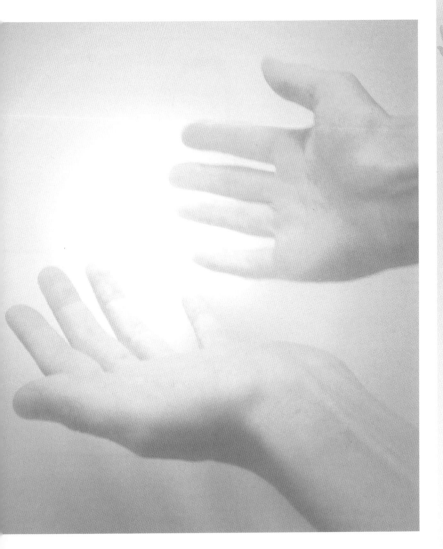

ABOVE When preparing for the Third Degree, you
should work on raising your energy vibration on all levels.

Preparing to change your life

Once you have made the decision to be a Reiki Master, you should start to prepare for your life to change. If you are serious in your intent about the step you are about to take, you will understand that Reiki is no longer going to be a kind of spiritual accessory in your life – it is going to *be* your life. Being a Reiki Master is not so much a job as a vocation in which you will be who you truly are. Being a Reiki Master is not just about being good at giving classes and passing attunements; it is also about having the knowledge to 'go on a journey' with the person you are teaching, and acting as their guide.

There are several things you can do to help you prepare for training as a Master, whichever route you have chosen to take. These will help you to raise your energy vibration on all levels, from the physical to the spiritual, in preparation for the final attunement you will receive.

Practising regularly

Focus on the regularity of your practice. Daily self-healing treatments and meditation are advisable. You should also do as many treatment swaps as you can with other practitioners. This means you will be receiving Reiki regularly from sources other than yourself, as well as giving it to others who are experienced, which will increase your understanding of the energy as well as raising your vibrations. It is also important to meditate on the symbols and mantras to improve your understanding of them and your connection with them.

Using your knowledge and skills

You may want to consider what other knowledge and skills you can bring to being a Master. Experience of other practices, such as yoga and Chi Kung, will help you to have an appreciation of a physical approach to working with energy. Knowledge of various philosophies and religions will give you insights into the connectedness of belief systems, and reading books about a wide range of other healing methods will add to your understanding of various conditions and ways of treating them. All of these (and you can probably think of others) will contribute to a depth of knowledge that, while not mandatory as part of the training, ultimately makes for a more rounded Reiki Master.

Attunement is the beginning

Finally, it is important to remember that, when you receive the attunement making you a Reiki Master, this signifies the beginning of your journey, not the end.

Symbol 4 – DKM

The Master symbol, DKM, is not a symbol as such, but like HSZSN (see pages 170–171) is comprised of three *Kanji* that make up a sentence, which is also the mantra connected with the symbol. The symbol is used as part of the attunement process for all levels of Reiki, but is only taught at the third level.

The characteristic associated with the symbol in the Western teachings is simply that of Mastership, while in the Japanese teachings the characteristic is Empowerment. One of its functions is to give us a direct connection to the Master within us. This is the part of us that is already enlightened but hidden from us, waiting to be discovered through the journey of many spiritual practices. In other words, Reiki is not unique in helping us to access the Light within us, but is simply one path to travel.

Indeed, Symbol 4 has its origins in the Buddhist tradition, and can be found in a *Mikkyô* text of the Tendai Buddhism practised by Mikao Usui. It is used as part of an esoteric ritual in which the practitioner becomes One with their original Buddha nature, enabling them to manifest the Light within, which is a natural force of energy. This knowledge helps us to understand why Usui chose this symbol as the ultimate one in the development of a Reiki practice.

The Master symbol brings in energy of a higher vibration with intensified qualities of healing. It can be used with all the other symbols to intensify their power and to purify the intention behind them. This is a symbol that sheds light on all situations, whether physical, mental or spiritual, and clears all blockages in the way of resolving issues, no matter how deeply buried.

Meditating on the symbol develops our self-awareness and powers our spiritual growth. The symbol should be drawn using the same method as with the others – drawing it with the palm or the fingers, or visualizing it in the mind's eye. It is multi-dimensional in that it has the three dimensions of height, width and depth, and the added dimensions of operating in space and time. One suggested method of meditation with this symbol is to draw it and step into it as if you were in a hologram. During meditation it frequently appears to have different colours, violet being one of the most commonly experienced. You can also intuitively visualize it as having a colour when using it in a particular situation to intensify its energy.

RIGHT The Master symbol enables us to access the part of us that is already enlightened, but hidden from our awareness.

The mantra – DKM

There are many translations of the mantra, ranging from 'treasure house of the great beaming light' to 'great enlightenment' or 'great bright light'.

Light is the common characteristic of the translations, so you may want to focus on the concept of Light when chanting the mantra, using the same technique as described on pages 88–89.

Exercise to balance *Ki* 1

Reiki teachers need to be able to balance their energy. This Chi Kung exercise is an excellent daily exercise for promoting energetic balance and may be used by Reiki practitioners at any level.

Opening and closing the *Ki*

The most important aspect of this exercise is focusing on feelings of resistance. When you are pushing down the energy you could visualize pushing a swimming float under the water, and when pulling the energy up, imagine the backs of your hands are attached to the floor by an elastic substance.

1 Stand with your feet shoulder-width apart and your knees slightly bent. Keep your eyes straight ahead and drop your shoulders. You should feel as though your crown and root chakras are aligned (these are called *Baihui* and *Huiyin* points in Chi Kung). Place the tip of your tongue against your hard palate, just behind your teeth. This is important in helping the *Ki* to make a complete circuit in the body.

2 Inhaling, bring your arms in front of your body, palms up.

3 Continuing on this in-breath, raise your arms to just below chest height. Your fingertips should not touch, and should be pointing towards one another. Your hands should be loosely flexed with the fingers open.

4 Rotate your arms inwards so that your palms are facing down.

5 Exhaling, press your hands down slowly. As you push downwards, allow your body to bend a little. Keep pushing down until you reach the navel area.

Repeat the sequence 4–6 times. Be careful not to bring your hands above chest height, as raising the energy above that level can cause mental imbalance. The key is balancing the energy around the navel or *Hara* area.

Exercise to balance *Ki* 2

The next exercise is particularly useful to teachers and is used by some as part of the attunement process. The exercise here is a simplified version of an advanced Chi Kung exercise. You may have to practise it several times before you start to have any sensation of the energy flowing around the entire circuit. One way to solve this is by mentally taking the energy around until you become aware of the physical sensation.

The microcosmic orbit
You can either sit or stand for this exercise. Personally, I feel standing makes the exercise easier until you are familiar with it.

1 Stand with your feet shoulder-width apart. Your knees should be slightly bent as though you were perched on a high stool. Keep your eyes straight ahead and drop your shoulders. You should feel as though your crown and root chakras are aligned (these are called *Baihui* and *Huiyin* points in Chi Kung). Place the tip of your tongue against your hard palate, just behind your teeth. This is important in helping the *Ki* to make a complete circuit in the body. Keep your eyes completely or partially closed to aid you in feeling the energy.

2 First take the energy from the point just below your navel to your perineum, the point between the anus and the genitals, and contract the energy there. This means squeezing the muscles together, which gives the sensation of them lifting up inside the body. Women will be familiar with this technique if they have ever done Kegel exercises at childbirth classes.

3 Now take the energy from the perineum to the base of your spine, and from there guide the energy up your spine, past the back of the heart to the neck and up the back of the head to the crown. Now visualize the energy flowing down from the crown to the tongue, which, placed against the roof of the mouth, connects the two circuits. The energy can now flow down the centre of the body back to the perineum.

Repeat this circuit 4–6 times initially. If the energy is getting stuck in your head area, causing dizziness or headache, take the energy down to your feet and let it flow into the earth.

ABOVE The process of attunement reconnects the student to the Universal energy for the rest of their life.

Giving attunements

One of the central functions of a Reiki teacher is performing the ritual of initiating others by giving them attunements (see pages 96–97). Initiation rituals are found in other spiritual traditions to greater or lesser degrees of significance, but it is a central aspect of Reiki because students cannot practise the method without receiving the attunements. Attunements are intended to reconnect the student to the spiritual energy of the Universe, and at the same time raise their personal energy levels. The latter helps them to be a stronger channel for the Reiki energy.

Methods of giving attunements

Teachers have different methods of giving the attunements. For example, teachers from the Reiki Alliance give four separate attunements at the first level, and one attunement each at the second and third levels. Teachers from other schools may only give one attunement at each level.

There are also numerous variations in the physical method the teacher uses. In all the methods, the student is usually seated with eyes closed and hands in prayer position, but some teachers may touch the body, moving around the person from back to front and finishing at the back, and other teachers may not touch the body at all. All the methods only take minutes to complete.

The important thing to remember is that there is no right or wrong way to give attunements – they all work as long as the intention of the Reiki Master is clear.

Practice makes perfect

As a teacher, you will need to practise the attunement technique you have been taught until you can do it almost without thinking. Confidence in your physical technique will allow you to focus more on the energetic aspect of the process when you come to teach a class. If you make a mistake, such as miss out strokes of a symbol, I suggest that, rather than stop and start again, you have the intention for the mistake to be corrected. It is my belief that if your intention is for the attunement to take place, and you go through the process in a respectful manner, the student will always receive the attunement and draw the energy to them that they need. It is also good to remember that the energy experienced in an attunement is not dependent on the 'power' of the teacher but on the needs of the student.

No going back

Finally, once the student has received the initiation it cannot be removed. There is no such thing as a temporary attunement – once given, it is there for life.

A professional practice

Some students make the decision to become a professional Reiki practitioner. You don't need to have the Third Degree to do this, nor, strictly speaking, the Second, although it is undoubtedly beneficial to have reached this level as your experience with the energy will improve your treatment skills.

It is perhaps wise to start off on a small scale, combining your professional practice with your regular job, if you have one. In this way, you can build up a client list gradually and at the same time discover whether it is something you will enjoy doing full time. There are considerable advantages to keeping it part time in that you can have two professions. I know of a very successful lawyer who, in the evenings, turns one of his offices into a Reiki treatment room, much to the bemusement of the other partners in his firm. In this way, his life is fulfilled in all ways, and he is able to keep costs down, passing that benefit on to his clients.

Finding a place to practise

Starting off in your own home is the best idea if your family is supportive, or you can schedule treatments so they don't conflict with family commitments. Alternatively, you could go to your clients' homes. Although this sounds a promising solution, you should consider the fact that you will not be able to prepare the space in the same way as you would elsewhere, and you will have very little control over the rest of the environment, such as noise of other people, pets and telephones. These will all work against a relaxing experience.

Another option is to hire a room in an alternative therapy practice or a beauty salon. You may be able to rent a room for just a few hours a week and so share the costs with other practitioners (otherwise this can be an expensive route to take). Ideally, you need to have built up a good client list beforehand, or you will end up paying for hours when you have no clients. If you do decide on this route, do some research first into the success of the existing business and spend some time getting a good feel for the ethos and ambience of the place. The room you are going to work in should feel energetically right for you. If you have any misgivings about the room or the business, follow your instinct, even if it appears to be a good solution in other ways.

RIGHT There are many decisions to make when starting a professional practice. Follow your intuition and your heart when making them.

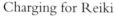

Charging for Reiki

Deciding what to charge for Reiki is an issue that many a professional practitioner struggles with. One way to approach it is to remember that money is simply a convenient method that we use in our society for the exchange of goods and services. Charging a fee puts a value on yourself and Reiki, which the client can respect. For their part, paying for Reiki shows respect for themselves as well, so the system of charging provides balance in giving and receiving.

You will need to do some research into the fees of other Reiki practitioners

BELOW Charging for Reiki allows both parties to show respect and balances the energy of giving and receiving.

in your area, and it is helpful to look at the charges of massage therapists, aromatherapists and reflexologists as well. This will give you a good idea of the going rate. It is a mistake to undercut the charges of other practitioners in your area. First, it will not necessarily bring you more clients because it may raise questions about why you are so cheap. Second, it will not win you any friends among the local practitioner community, and they may be a useful source of client referrals.

Settle on a charge that covers any costs involved in your practice, that you feel comfortable with and that is in line with other therapists' charges. If you feel the need to give 'free' treatments, offer them where they will be most beneficial, such as at a hospice.

Marketing your practice

Advertising regularly in local papers is expensive. It is better to look for a specialist alternative health directory, but even this may not prove to be a cost-effective way of building your business. Using the internet to publicize your practice is a cheaper and more effective option. You don't need to have your own website, simply add your contact details to some of the many web directories for practitioners.

One essential marketing item is a well-designed and written leaflet that tells people about Reiki, your background, treatment length, charges and contact details. These can be distributed in places you have researched that attract potential clients, such as health food shops, leisure centres, cafés and bookshops. A business card is also useful to have on hand when you are at professional events and social occasions.

Insurance and accounts

There are few costs involved in setting up a Reiki practice – your treatment table and marketing materials are the two key ones. However, you will also need insurance to cover you for public liability and indemnity, even if you are working at home. A number of insurers specialize in policies for various types of therapies; alternatively, you may be able to buy it from one of the umbrella Reiki organizations in your country.

Finally, you will also need to keep basic accounts, which should show earnings and expenditure on any items or transport costs related to your business.

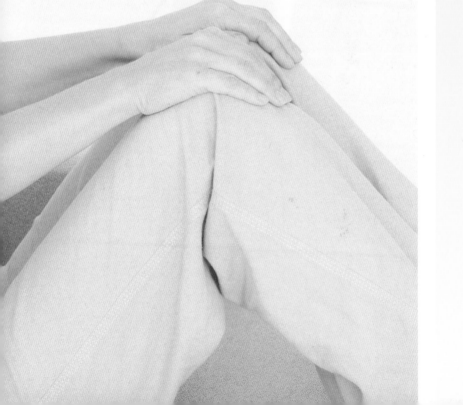

PART 4
Reiki hand positions

Patting and stroking

When Mikao Usui first started to show students how to use Reiki on themselves and on other people, he did not follow the structured system of hand positions that we are familiar with today. As we know, it was Chujiro Hayashi who formalized these at Usui's request. Usui used techniques of patting and stroking when giving a treatment. You may wish to use these in treatments and classes in addition to the hand positions. However, these techniques are optional. They are included to give you a more comprehensive idea of the way that Reiki has been practised.

Patting (*Uchite chiryô-hô*)

This patting technique can be used on areas where energy feels blocked, and will help it to flow again. It is similar to the Chi Kung technique of tapping the body to release stagnant energy that tends to accumulate in joint areas.

Using the flat of the hand, start off with a gentle, rhythmic patting of the area, gradually building the force up until it becomes a mild slapping action. Continue this until you feel the energy has released.

Patting

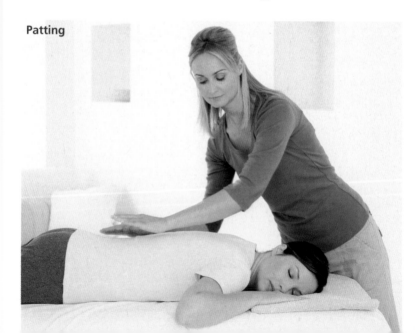

Stroking

Stroking (*Nadete chiryô-hô*)
This soothing technique encourages
energy flow around the body and is also
used to increase the flow of Reiki into and
through the body.

You can use this technique on both the
front and back of the person, but make
sure that you are always working in a
downwards motion. For example, you can
work from the shoulders down the arms,
and then from the shoulders to the waist.
After this, you can work from the waist to
the toes. Be careful not to touch the
breasts or genitals.

Place both hands flat on the body.
Applying enough pressure on each
stroke to prevent the person having
the sensation of being tickled, stroke
your hands down the body, using
short rather than long strokes, and
have the intention for the flow of
energy to increase.

Hand positions
for self-treatment

The simplicity of the system for treating
yourself makes it possible for you to
self-treat wherever you are. Whether you
are travelling or at home, your hands are
always available.

Treating yourself

Whether you decide to sit or lie down to give yourself a treatment, always make sure that you are comfortable. If possible, turn off any potential distractions such as your mobile phone.

What follows are the set positions for a self-treatment, and you should follow the order shown here. At times, you may want to deviate from this and concentrate on a specific area. There is nothing wrong with this, although it is always better to treat the whole body as regularly as possible. Similarly, if you don't have time to give yourself a full treatment, you may find that focusing on the kidney area and the head is enough to refresh you.

Beginners often worry about holding the positions for the length of time specified in the instructions. Rather than concern yourself with time, pay more attention to what your hands are telling you and follow them. If your hands feel glued to a spot, keep them in a position as long as you are having that sensation. You will probably find that the length of time you take to give yourself a treatment will vary, but as a rule of thumb it should be around 45 minutes.

You may find that if you give yourself a Reiki treatment last thing at night that you will fall asleep before you complete half of the treatment session. This is not a problem and does not affect the benefits Reiki brings you. However, if you want to make sure that you give yourself a full treatment, after waking might be a better alternative.

LEFT Giving yourself Reiki every day is one way to show respect for yourself as well as keeping yourself in peak condition. Wherever you are, whatever you are doing, place your hands on yourself and bless yourself with Reiki energy.

Position 1

Make sure you are in a comfortable position, and that you won't be disturbed before you start treating yourself.

Place your hands over your face with your palms over your eyes and the upper part of your cheeks. Your fingertips should be just above your hairline, and your fingers and thumbs should be kept close together. Hold the position for at least three minutes.

Position 1

Position 2

This position is a good one to use on its own if you have earache or if you are having problems with your teeth.

Cup your hands over your ears, still keeping your fingers together. Hold the position until you feel ready to move on. If you have toothache, you can also cup your hands over your jaw.

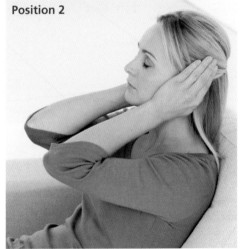

Position 2

Position 3

Position 3

Although this position can be done quite easily sitting up, as seen here, it is easier to do when lying down as there is less strain on the arms.

Cup the back of your head with your hands placed horizontally across the skull. Your fingers will be pointing in opposite directions.

Alternative Position 3

Alternatively, place your hands together, fingers pointing upwards and palms at the base of the skull.

Position 4a and 4b

Position 4 can only be done by those with Second Degree Reiki, as it involves drawing Symbols 1 and 2 (CKR and SHK) on the forehead.

Position 4a Keep your left hand on the back of your head in a position that is comfortable for you and does not involve twisting your wrist around. Using your right hand, draw the symbols on the centre of your forehead.

Position 4b Next place this hand across your forehead, covering it completely.

Position 4a

Position 4b

Position 5

Position 5

There are two versions of this position for treating the throat area. Use whichever you find most comfortable, and again hold the position until you are ready to move on.

Keeping your fingers together, place your left hand around the back of your neck. Then loosely cup your right hand around the front of your throat area, with your thumb pointing towards your right ear. You can reverse this if you wish.

Alternative Position 5

Alternatively, hold this position by cupping both of your hands together in front of your neck, with your fingertips going just behind and under your ears.

Positions 6a and 6b

These two positions treat the stomach, the spleen and the liver, and are useful on their own if your stomach is feeling upset or if you feel that the spleen and liver need some help in getting rid of body toxins.

Position 6a For the first body position, place your hands across the solar plexus area, with palms down and fingertips touching in the middle. Remember to keep your fingers together.

Position 6b When you have finished giving Reiki here, move your hands down, keeping them in the same position, so that your middle fingers are just above your navel, and give Reiki to this area.

Position 6a

Position 6b

Position 7

Position 8

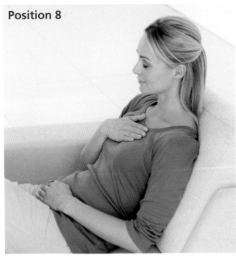

Position 7

This position treats the pelvic and reproductive areas and the reproductive organs. It is a good position for women to use when their period is starting as it will help to relieve any cramping pain.

Place the heels of your palms on each of your hip bones and point your fingers down and into the middle so that your fingertips touch. You can keep your thumbs in close to your hands or spread them outwards, making a heart shape between your hands.

Position 8

The last of the front body positions is one that helps to balance the energy. This is the position that I use before starting to give a Reiki treatment to another person.

Place one hand over the *Hara* or second chakra area, just below the navel, and the other over the fourth chakra, which is beside the physical heart in the centre of the breastbone area.

Positions 9a and 9b

Clearly, there is no way that you can comfortably treat the whole of your back by yourself. Instead, self-treatment on the back focuses on the kidneys and the adrenals just above the kidneys. For both of these positions, place the palms of your hands on each side of your back with your fingers pointing into your spine. If your back is not very broad your fingertips will touch.

Position 9a To cover the adrenals, place the outside edge of your hands slightly over the bottom of your ribcage and your hands will naturally be in place.

Position 9b To cover the kidneys, slide your hands down one hand's width to rest on the lower waist.

Position 9a

Position 9b

Position 10

Position 10

The shoulders are the only other back areas that are reasonably accessible, and as we store so much tension in them it is a good idea to give them Reiki whenever we can. This is a good position to use while you take a break from working on a computer or while you are watching television.

The position can be done in two ways. Cross your arms in front of you and place your hands on the back of each shoulder.

Alternative Position 10

Alternatively, instead of crossing your arms in front of you, put your right hand over the back of your right shoulder and your left hand behind your left shoulder, pointing your fingers towards your spine.

Positions 11 and 12

These positions are additional and are not taught by the traditional Usui Masters as part of a self-treatment. They can easily be done in the bath or as part of a foot massage or reflexology treatment.

Position 11 The first is giving Reiki to your knees. The knees can hold stagnant energy and fear, as well as being problem areas for people with arthritis and rheumatism. I have included them in the full self-treatment, but they can be done separately. Place your hands on your knees and hold the position for three minutes.

Position 12 Similarly, your feet and ankles, which do so much hard work, can be treated by simply placing your hands around them in a way that is comfortable for you.

Position 11

Position 12

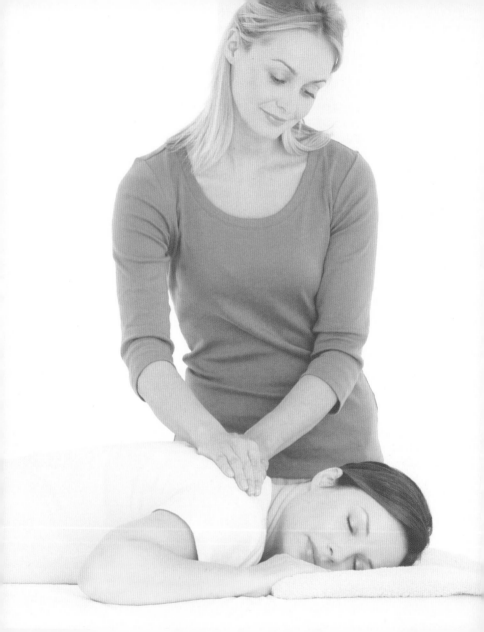

Hand positions
for treating others

Treating others is a privilege and a profound
experience in many ways. Using your
intuition and listening to your hands is
more important than following the hand
positions precisely.

Treating others

A typical Reiki treatment given to another person usually lasts about an hour if each hand position is held for the minimum of three minutes. There are times when you may wish to spend longer on a treatment, perhaps if the person is particularly unwell, you intuitively feel that they need more time in general, or you want to focus on a particular area.

If you are giving a treatment for the first time, you will need to allow extra time before the session begins to discuss the treatment with them and answer any questions they may have. I often allow an extra half hour for a first treatment with a new client so that there is ample time before and after to cover any concerns and discuss any experiences they had during the treatment.

Importance of the head

The first five positions are on the head and throat area. I find that with some people I may spend almost half of the treatment time working on the head, especially in the first few treatments. Since the head is the location of the spirit-centred chakras, the intellect and the main organizers of the endocrine system – the pituitary and pineal glands – it is logical that this area requires extra attention. However, it varies according to the needs of each recipient.

Flowing movements

Regular practice at giving treatments to others will ensure that the transition between hand positions is smooth. Having self-confidence and controlling your breathing will help to make your movements flow. This makes for a more relaxing experience for you both.

LEFT You may want to allow time for discussion before and after a Reiki treatment.

Positions 1a and 1b

These positions help you to tune into another person's energy flow.

Position 1a Have the recipient lie comfortably on their back on the treatment table, hands by their sides, not folded over the stomach, and seat yourself behind their head. As a starting point, rest your hands gently on their shoulders for a few moments. This helps you to tune into their energy flow.

Position 1b Place your hands together, with the sides of your thumbs touching and palms facing downwards, a few centimetres above the recipient's face. Slowly lower your hands onto the face. Ensure that your thumbs are placed in the middle of the forehead and slightly over the top of the bridge of the nose. Then place your palms over the eyes and lightly rest your fingers on the cheeks. Hold the position for three minutes.

Position 1a

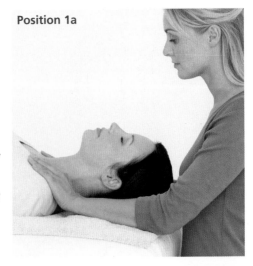

Position 1b

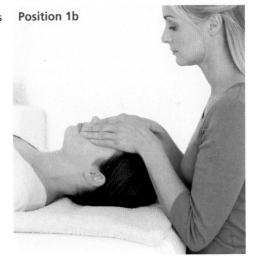

Position 2a

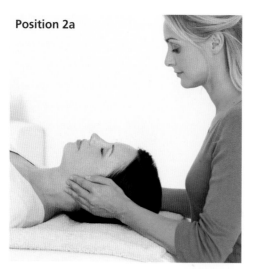

Position 2b

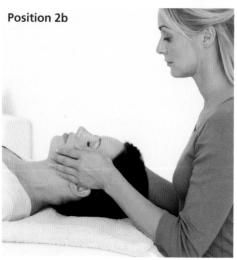

Positions 2a and 2b

There are variations on some of the positions, depending on the preference of the Master. Shown here are two variations on the second position, both of which were taught to me by Masters of the traditional school. The first position is Hawayo Takata's, and the second is a commonly found variation.

Position 2a Place the palms of your hands over each of the recipient's ears, with your thumbs in front of the ears. Your fingers should fall into a natural position over the back of the jaw and neck.

Position 2b Place the heel of your palm above each temple with your palms over the temples. Your fingers should lie against the side of the face, with the little fingers resting in front of each ear.

Position 3a

Positions 3a, 3b, and 3c

It takes some practice to manoeuvre your hands gracefully into these positions. Breathe into your centre and don't rush it. Many recipients feel tense when you are manoeuvring them into this position and are unable to allow you to fully support their head and neck. Encourage them to let you take the weight of their head, but don't mention it too many times or they will become more self-conscious. Relaxed or not, this is a favourite position for many people, probably because it echoes the way a mother holds a baby's head. After a treatment, some people have singled out this position as the one that makes them feel 'very cared for'.

Position 3a Slide your right hand from over the recipient's ear onto the side of their cheek. Place your left hand on the left side of the recipient's face and slowly push the head over to the right, so that the back of your right hand is now touching the table.

Position 3b

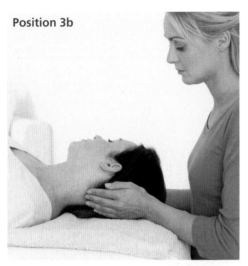

Position 3b Now place your left hand under the back of the head with your fingers pointing down and over part of the neck.

Position 3c

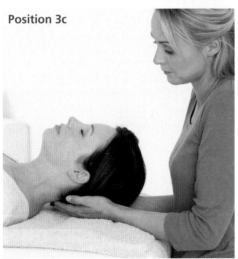

Position 3c Slowly roll the recipient's head over to the left so that the back of your left hand is touching the table and their head is supported in your left palm. Bring your right hand in under the back of the head so that your hands are cradling the head and the top of the neck. Make sure your hands are comfortable and that the recipient's head feels secure and balanced.

Position 4a

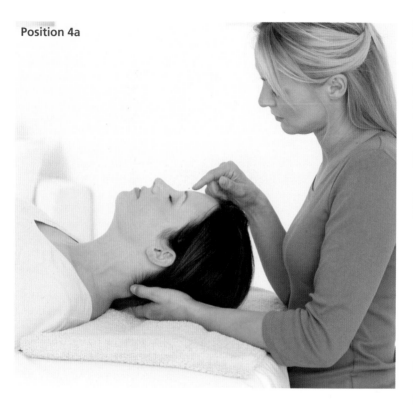

Positions 4a and 4b

This position entails using the symbols for mental healing as taught in the Second Degree. These are drawn over the centre of the forehead. With both hands under the head as in position 3c (see page 221), choose which hand you will use to draw the symbols.

Position 4a From position 3c, slide your chosen hand down the back of the recipient's neck to support it, while you move your other hand into the centre back of their head. When you have the head supported, remove your chosen hand from the back of the head and draw the symbols over the centre of the forehead.

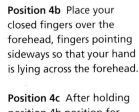

Position 4b

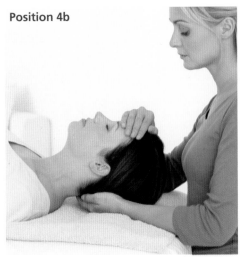

Position 4c

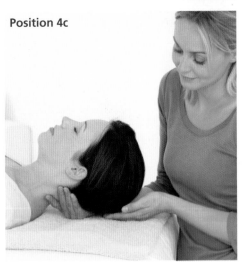

Position 4b Place your closed fingers over the forehead, fingers pointing sideways so that your hand is lying across the forehead.

Position 4c After holding position 4b position for 3–5 minutes, first remove your hand from the forehead and slip it back under the neck. This provides support while you slowly slide your other hand out from under the head, pulling your hand towards you.

The recipient may again lift their head to help you with this movement; quietly tell them to relax and let you do the work.

Positions 5a and 5b

Some people find it uncomfortable to have another person's hands too close to their throat, and you should consider this when deciding how to treat this area. Also remember that the throat is an area that holds an enormous amount of emotional issues for many people, and during treatment some very strong images, emotions and even pain can surface.

Position 5a First rest your elbows on either side of the recipient's head (but not too close) and bring your hands in front of the throat area, approximately 7.5 cm (3 in) away from the throat. Interlace your fingers with the tips of your thumbs just touching (it doesn't matter if they don't) and cup the jawline and throat area. There are variations on this position. Simply lay your hands on each side of the recipient's jaw with your thumbs just above the jawbone and your fingers pointing towards each other, but not interlaced. This version brings your hands closer to the throat area, while in the position shown your hands should be kept some distance from the throat.

Position 5b Finish by unlacing your fingers and pulling your arms away in an arc until they reach the edge of the table.

Position 5a

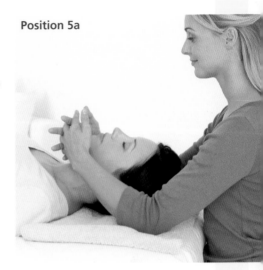

Position 5b

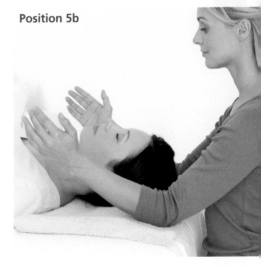

Position 6

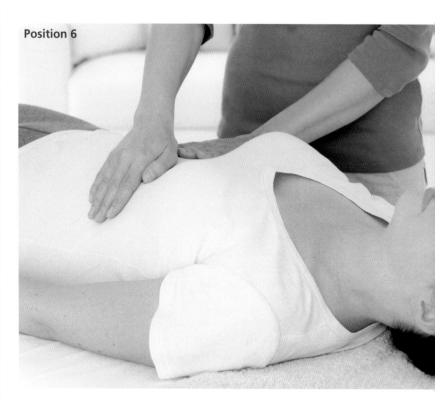

Position 6

Having finished the recipient's head and throat area, you move on to treat the rest of the front of their body. To do these positions, you will need to stand up unless you have the type of office chair that moves around on castors.

For the first body position, place your hands one behind the other beneath the chest area (on a woman, just below the breasts), across the ribs. Hold the position for three minutes.

Position 7

Use the version of this position that feels most appropriate.

To move from Position 6 into this one, you can either keep your hands in the same position and just slide them 2.5–5 cm (1–2 in) down the recipient's body, or you can slide the hand farthest from you towards you and down the body, while sliding the hand nearest to you across to the other side. You can use this crisscross motion on the back and front of the body.

Alternative Positions 6 and 7

An alternative way to do the sixth and seventh positions is to start by placing your hands together on one side of the recipient's body, holding the position for three minutes, then slide both your hands over to the other side of the body. What is important with both methods is that you cover the chakras and major organs.

Position 7

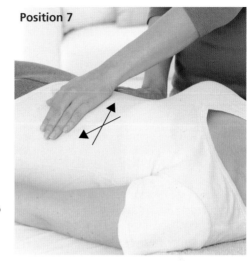

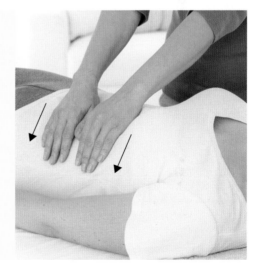

Position 8

This position treats the pelvic area. As you are working near the genitals, you will need to show sensitivity and avoid any direct contact with the genitals themselves. The position shown here is most suitable for working with women.

Place your left hand on the inner side of the recipient's right hip bone, fingers together and pointing down towards the pubic bone. Then place the heel of your right hand a small distance from your left fingertips, pointing your hand upwards on the inner side of the left hip bone so that your hands are making a V-shape.

Alternative Position 8 for working with men

Instead of placing your hands in a V-shape across the pelvic area, it is better to place a hand on, or just inside, each hip bone. The easiest way to do this is to place one hand with the fingers facing straight up, and place the other with the fingers facing down. Being careful in this area will avoid any embarrassment on either you or your client's part.

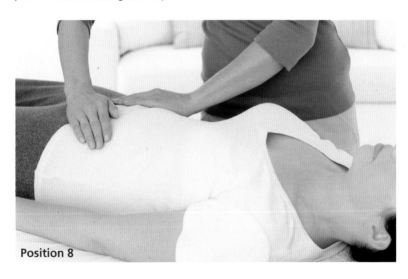

Position 8

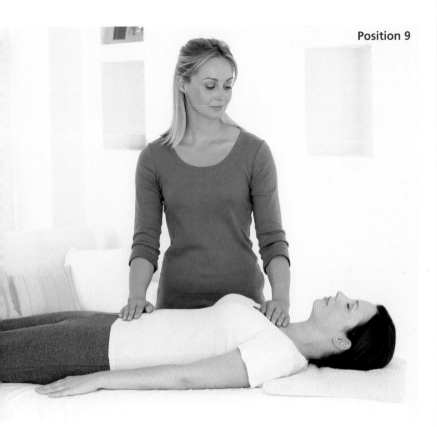

Position 9

This position concludes treating the front of the body by balancing and linking the energy in the upper and lower sections. This position works with the sacral and heart chakras.

Place your right hand on the recipient's abdomen and your left hand on the breastbone, fingers pointing to the head. Stay in this position for 3–5 minutes or until you feel the energy is in balance between your hands.

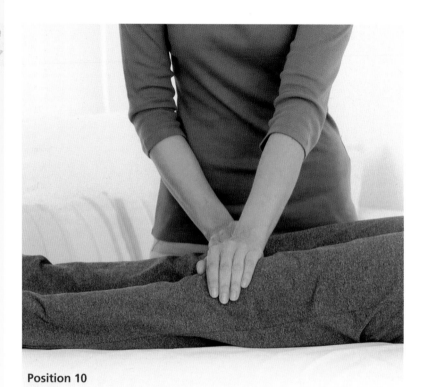

Position 10

Positions 10 and 11

These positions are additional and were not taught by Hawayo Takata. Use these positions if you feel they are appropriate to the needs of the recipient, or use them to find out the sequence of treatment positions that you think works best for most recipients.

Position 10 The first position treats the knees. You move from the pelvic position to this position, one hand at a time. Hold the position for three minutes.

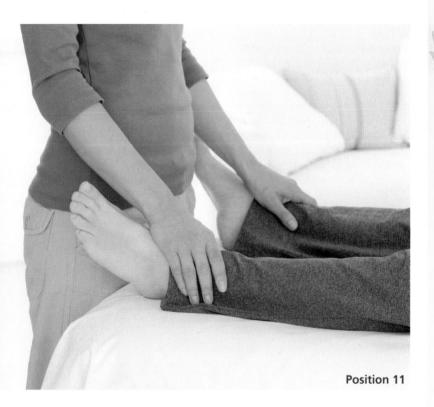

Position 11

Position 11 Stand at the bottom of the table and move your hands down to the ankles and feet, holding them with your hands pointing upwards. Next ask the recipient to turn over onto their stomach. As most recipients are very relaxed by now, tell them to turn over slowly. You can arrange their hands by their sides,

although some people prefer to rest their head on their arms. This is fine, but it does make it more difficult for you to do the first back position, as their muscles are scrunched up. One solution is to ask them to keep their arms by their sides just while you do the first position.

Position 12

The shoulders hold a lot of tension for most people. Some recipients' shoulders feel like sponges, soaking up energy, and you may find that your hands don't want to move. This feeling of your hands being glued into a position can occur at any time during a Reiki treatment, so it is best just to stay in the position until your hands feel ready to move, as that area of the body obviously needs extra energy.

This position is also a good one to use on its own with the person seated. For example, if one of your family has been working at a computer for long hours, you can encourage them to take a break and give them ten minutes of Reiki on the shoulders and back of the neck. You can also combine this position with giving a head massage.

Lay your hands across the recipient's shoulders, in the same way as on the front of their body. I find it slightly easier on my hands in a straight line, but instead allow them to curve a little so that one hand is pointing slightly upwards and the other downwards.

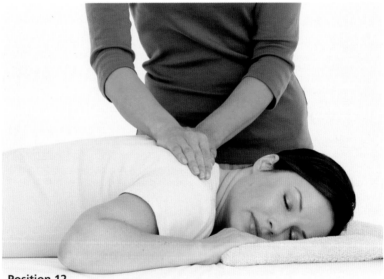

Position 12

Position 13

Treating the back of the heart area may produce some interesting sensations and you might feel inclined to spend more time here than usual when treating some people. As everyone is unique and you never know in advance what you might feel, listen with your hands at all times.

Move your hands from the shoulders down to the back of the heart area and hold for three minutes. This is an area that may require some extra attention. You are also covering the lungs at this point, so it is worth spending some more time here if necessary. You may find that you sense different emotional responses in the recipient around the heart area. Sometimes they will be aware of these and mention them, while with some people you alone may feel what is going on. Depending on the length of a person's back, you may be able to fit in another hand position over the area just below the heart, before moving on to the adrenals and the kidneys.

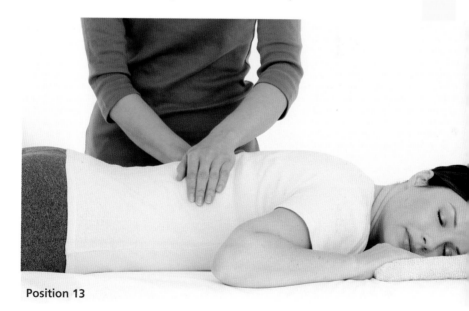

Position 13

Position 14

To cover the adrenals and kidneys completely, you will probably need to do this position in stages.

Move your hands down the recipient's back from the previous position, first covering their adrenals, and then move your hands down again and cover their kidneys. If the recipient has back pain around the tail end of the spine, you may want to keep moving your hands down until you have covered the whole area. If your recipient is male, you can treat the prostate gland by placing one of your hands on top of the other in the centre of his buttocks, just below the tailbone, after you have completed the back sessions.

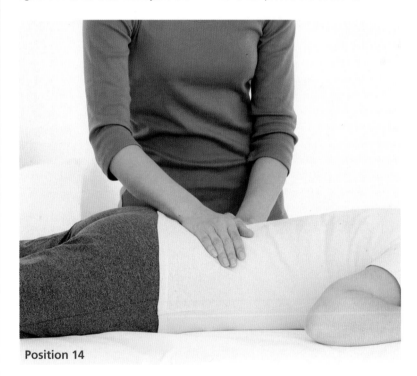

Position 14

Position 15a

Position 15

This final position grounds the recipient and needs to be done in two stages, treating each side of the body in turn.

Some people, myself included at times, experience quite dramatic sensations with this position. I remember receiving treatments where I felt that I had expanded to fill the room, and it was only when the practitioner got to this position that I felt as if I was filling my 'normal' space again. Similarly, if I felt my energy was unbalanced during a treatment in terms of right and left sides, this position equalized it again.

Position 15a Place one of your hands at the top of the recipient's leg nearest to you and place your other hand flat against the sole of their foot. Hold this position for three minutes.

Position 15b Stand at the other side of the table to treat the other leg. When I move around the bottom of the table to get to the other side, I hold onto one of the recipient's feet so that contact is not lost. Repeat the position on the recipient's other leg and foot. It is possible to lean across the table to do both stages of this position, provided you don't find it puts strain on your back.

Clearing the aura

Now that you have finished the treatment, all that remains is to clear the aura and help the recipient to feel grounded before she gets up. Smoothing down an aura after a treatment helps the energy to settle down and can also remove any negative energy. There are many ways to clear the aura and I have tried several of them. Shown here is the method of the traditional school.

Smoothing down the aura

The method I use starts on the physical body itself, finishing off by working in the outer layers of the aura.

1 Place your hands on the sides of the recipient's hips and pull firmly down to their feet. Shake off the excess energy from your hands. Do this three times.

1

2 Then place your hands on their back, around the waist area. Push your hands up towards the heart, outwards over each shoulder and down the outside of the arms. Shake off the excess energy from your hands. Do this three times.

3 Now, working with your hands about 30 cm (1 ft) away from the body, smooth off the aura itself. Start at the crown of the head and work down to the feet.

2

3

Finishing off

Having smoothed down the aura, I place my hand in the centre of the recipient's back and gently rub it in a circular motion. Sometimes I also say their name softly if they are having trouble coming round. The more relaxed a person is during the treatment, the longer it takes to rouse them. When you have done this, you can then bring water to the recipient. You should advise them to

drink as much water as possible for the next day or two, as this will help to remove toxins more rapidly.

Once the recipient has roused, I leave the room quietly so that they can get up in their own time (but with an elderly person, or somebody with balance or back problems, it is best to stay and help them get up from the treatment table). I then wash my hands to finish the session symbolically and clear myself of any of the recipient's energy. You can do a more extended cleansing as described on pages 180–181 once the person has left, or at the end of the day if you have multiple sessions booked close together.

Talking about the treatment

Just after being roused is the point at which most clients either want to relate their experiences during the treatment, or ask what you felt. They want to know if you could feel blockages in their body, and whether you can tell if there is anything wrong. This is when you need to exercise caution and sensitivity. It is not easy to interpret energy sensations as they don't always mean the same thing. My interpretation of a cold sensation around the kidneys might be completely different to another practitioner's. Added to this, the meaning of a sensation I feel in one client may have an entirely different meaning in another client, yet feel similar.

Remember that you must not make any diagnosis. Instead, talk in general terms about what they felt in different areas of the body and whether they have had any problems there before. In this way, you can guide them towards their own conclusions.

Case study: the insomniac

I had a wonderful client who had come for treatment for insomnia. He was quite convinced that Reiki would not do any good, but his wife had asked him to give it a try, and so he arrived for his first treatment. After ten minutes he was fast asleep, and by the end of the treatment he was in an even deeper sleep. I finally managed to wake him by rubbing his back, using firmer strokes than usual. He said that it was the best sleep he had experienced in a while, and from then on he became one of my most regular clients.

Patterns of healing

Responses following a treatment vary from person to person. Some people experience an incredible burst of physical energy, while others feel the need to go home and sleep. My neighbour, who lived upstairs, asked me for a treatment during a bout of flu. After the treatment, she went home and a short while later I heard sounds of a lot of activity upstairs. The next day I asked her what she had been doing and she told me that she had felt so energized after the treatment that she had decided to rearrange all the furniture in the apartment. Another told me that he went home and brought out all the music he had listened to in his 20s and danced to it for hours.

On the other hand, some people may return to you and tell you that they felt very tired, or that they experienced mood swings for a few days following the treatment. As a practitioner, you should not take this as an indication that the treatment was not successful. This is simply the response of that person on that particular occasion. You can explain to them that we all have different responses, although you cannot explain to them why they happened to have that experience.

If the person appears to be a bit 'spaced out' or dizzy after the treatment, make sure that they are grounded before they leave. This is especially necessary if they are going to drive straight away. You can do this using part of the grounding exercise on pages 152–153. Get them to sit with their feet flat on the floor and visualize the energy pouring out through the soles of their feet into the ground. Stamping the feet on the floor is another quick way of grounding energy.

How many treatments?

The next thing to consider is the number of treatments a person needs. This very much depends on the condition that is being treated. Reiki can be used to treat both acute and chronic conditions. An acute condition is one that is temporary, such as cuts, colds and viral infections. Headaches are also acute unless they are frequent, in which case they are a sign of an underlying chronic condition. Chronic conditions are long-term ones, such as arthritis. However, many chronic conditions also have acute episodes, asthma and eczema being two typical examples.

RIGHT It is important to ensure that a person is grounded after a treatment and that they do not leave without feeling 'earthed'.

Acute conditions

These may respond well after only one or two treatments. I used to suffer from flu regularly and found it very difficult to recover every time. Just before I learnt Reiki, I caught yet another bout of flu and asked a friend who had just become a Reiki practitioner if she would give me a treatment. As she gave me Reiki, I felt my body become heavier and heavier until I felt as if I had turned into a block of concrete. This sensation was followed by one of this heaviness flowing into the floor I was lying on. When the treatment had finished, I expected to feel a little better. However, the flu had gone in that one session, and I felt even better than before I had become ill. In fact, after I had taken the Second Degree class, I stopped contracting flu altogether.

You will probably find that with an acute condition, such as a cold or flu, the best approach is to give treatments frequently within a short period. This is easier to do with family than with clients attending a Reiki practice, as you are on hand at home to give treatments as often as needed. Always give a full treatment every time, and if required extra treatment on specific areas.

Chronic conditions

These require a longer-term approach. The root causes of a chronic condition form at the level of mind and spirit before manifesting as physical symptoms. For example, the causes of chronic conditions appearing in later life have been forming for some time. Therefore it is unlikely that the causes can be removed quickly.

It is impossible to say exactly how many treatments a person with a chronic condition will need, but it is responsible to advise them that they will probably require many treatments. Ultimately it is their decision to continue or stop treatments, so one way to approach the query is to suggest they have some treatments and see how they get on with them.

With chronic conditions, you may want to tell the person that sometimes a condition gets worse before it gets better. Everyone has their own healing pattern, and while people often feel some immediate relief after the first treatment they may find that after the next few treatments their symptoms get worse. This is discouraging for them and they may wish to give up. It is then helpful for them to know that others have similar experiences, and that staying with the Reiki, perhaps supplemented with other therapies, will take them through the healing crisis.

LEFT The number of treatments needed depends on the nature of the condition being treated.

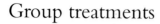

Group treatments

Taking part in a group treatment is a unique experience. We are so used to healing, orthodox or alternative, being given on a one-to-one basis that we have lost our sense of the power that working in groups can have. Many Reiki teachers hold meetings to give group treatments, but you can always start your own.

Organizing meetings

Decide how long you want the meetings to last, and how frequently you want to hold them. As a rule of thumb, about two hours should be enough, and twice monthly seems to be the most favoured interval. You may decide to rotate the meetings around various members' houses – this gives every group member the opportunity to be a group leader, and the experience of responsibility for the group.

Then consider how you want to structure the meetings. There should be room for each person to share their special gift. For example, one person may want to lead the group in a visualization, and another may have brought a piece of music they want to share. You could also start in a circle, simply sharing experiences. In this way, healing in the group can take many forms. You can then move on to the group treatment. Alternatively, you can start with the treatment.

Giving the group treatment

If you have a large number of people, consider dividing yourselves into two groups. You need to work on a time limit for each treatment, or you will be there for hours. So, for example, if there are six people and you have an hour to give the treatment, each person will have ten minutes. If one of the group has a special problem, you may decide to give that person some extra time.

Usually in a group treatment the recipient is treated lying on their back, unless they specifically want a treatment on their back. It is the responsibility of the group leader to sit at the head of the table and signal when to change hand positions, and when the treatment time for each person has finished.

The group leader will start with their hands in Position 1 (see page 221). The others place their hands on the part of the body nearest to them. They hold that position until the leader moves their hands to Position 2 (see page 222). There may not be room to move your hands very far, but the main thing to aim for is everybody moving their hands in unison.

RIGHT In a group treatment, the time that each person has is shorter than in a normal treatment, but the energy is intensified to the extent that is equivalent to a full-length individual treatment.

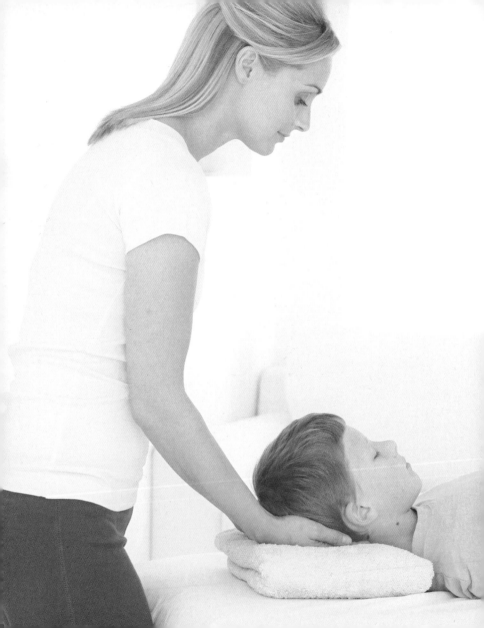

PART 5
Reiki for friends and family

Treating babies and children

Most children are very receptive to Reiki energy and find the concept of it magical, as it should be. Through children's programmes and books they are familiar with characters that have 'special powers', so it is not too much of a leap for their imaginations to accept the idea of healing a cut or getting to sleep more easily with energy coming through the hands.

Some children may resist receiving a treatment, and they have their own reasons for doing so. They are more sensitive to the energy than adults, so they are likely to be aware when you are giving them Reiki, even if you don't tell them what you are doing. In my opinion, if they don't want Reiki, respect that and stop giving it to them until they ask for it.

Older children are easier to work with as they have longer attention spans and more understanding of the idea of a structured process. With smaller children, you may have a problem getting them to stay still for long enough to receive a treatment, in which case you can treat them while they are sleeping.

Putting a child at ease

Sometimes involving a child in the process of setting up the room for the treatment is a way of focusing their attention on the treatment and making them feel more comfortable with the idea of lying on the table. One child I was treating would only get on the table after he had helped me light every candle he could find in the room. Once he was satisfied that was completed, he hopped up on the table.

Overall, children don't need to receive Reiki for as long as an adult. Their bodies are smaller and they have not accumulated the same energy blocks that adults have. A period of 20–30 minutes should be long enough for a full body treatment. You can treat a child lying down on the treatment table, but if they become restless let them sit up and talk to you while you continue giving them Reiki.

Attunements for parents and children

Ideally, parents who bring children for treatment should be encouraged to receive the attunements so that they can give Reiki to the child themselves. This is especially true if the child has a chronic condition that requires long-term treatment. It also gives the parents a sense of participating in their child's treatment. Don't forget that children can also receive the attunements themselves, and you should discuss this with your Reiki teacher.

RIGHT Children are very receptive to Reiki and giving regular treatments to your child offers you a unique way of bonding with them.

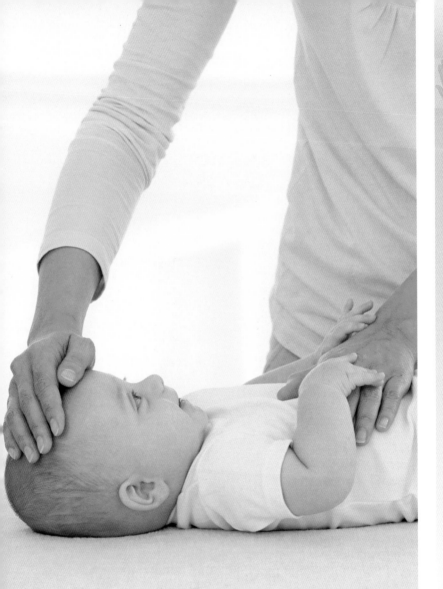

Treating children

Children are full of energy. You can feel this when you give them a Reiki treatment. The energy flows through the body effortlessly from head to toe as though there is nothing in the way. At least this is my experience with healthy children. However, this abundance of energy also means that it is sometimes difficult for them to settle down, especially at night. The steps that follow will help with this, and with aiding them to concentrate mentally.

Combining Reiki with a body relaxation exercise, such as one where you ask them to tighten and then relax every part of their body, working from the head down, can also be very effective for some children with sleep problems.

1

Calming

The focus of these treatments is on the head. This has the dual function of calming excess mental activity and releasing endorphins that make us feel happy. Smoothing down the aura will also help the energy to calm down.

1 Place one hand on the back of the head and the other across the forehead, covering the brow chakra. This position promotes calm and relieves stress.

2 Place both your hands under the back of the head, as though cradling it. This position promotes sleep in both children and adults.

3 Place one hand across the forehead and another on the solar plexus chakra. This helps to balance the emotions. You can, if you wish, continue by moving your hand from the solar plexus down to the stomach area. This will add to the child's feeling of relaxation.

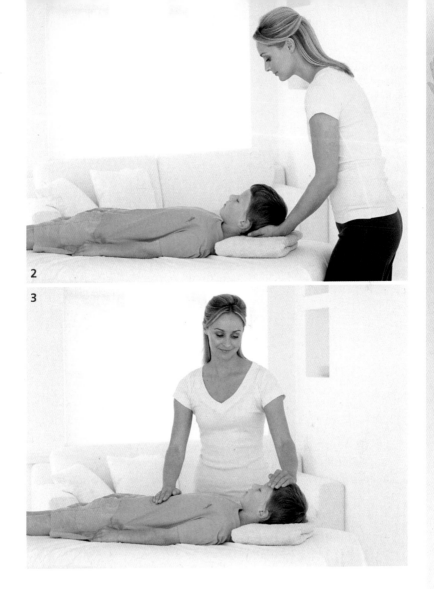

2

3

Increasing concentration

This is useful before exams or tests of any kind. Many children get more stressed than parents and teachers realize, and can even develop phobia-like symptoms about taking exams. This simple three-step treatment can help allay fears when used regularly. The hand positions help to calm mental activity and allow both mind and body to relax. Treatment may also help to bring about a positive change to the child's mental outlook on life, especially if they are supported by messages that encourage confidence.

1 Place your hands over the eyes, which should be closed. This draws the energy inwards.

2 Now place your hands on each side of the head in front of the ears. This balances the two sides of the brain.

3 Place both hands under the back of the head, as in step 2 of the previous exercise.

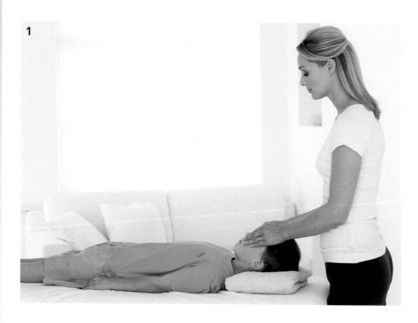

1

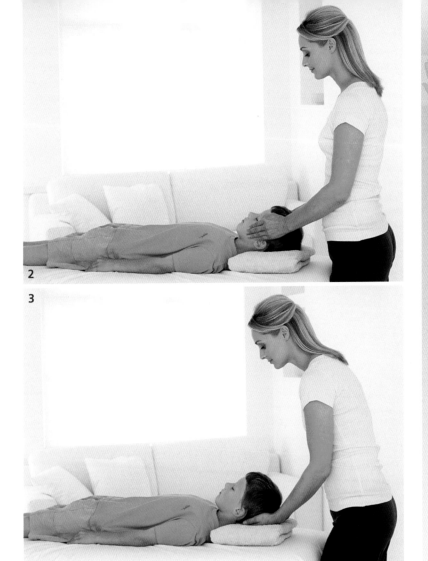

2

3

Treating babies

Reiki practitioners who are also new parents have a wonderful gift that will help them and their new baby through life, but especially through the first few weeks of bonding. Touch of any kind is incredibly important to a baby, and you will naturally have many opportunities during the course of the day to give your baby Reiki.

Like children, babies don't need full treatments, and you will probably find that even 10 minutes will be sufficient most of the time. If you find that your baby does not respond well to direct touch when giving Reiki, simply keep your hands above the body, as the Reiki will be absorbed just as well.

Reiki can be particularly useful in helping to establish a regular sleeping pattern, and it will also calm the baby when they are upset or restless or unable to sleep due to pain.

Getting to sleep

Because a baby's body is so small, you can usually give them a complete treatment while keeping your hands in just one position.

1 To help your baby go to sleep simply place one hand on their forehead and another on their stomach. Both these positions increase the feeling of security and relaxation.

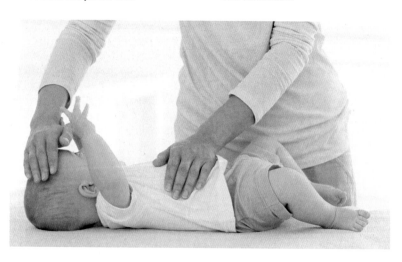

Total energy balance

This position helps to give your baby an overall feeling of calm and relaxation.

1 Either sit the baby up facing you, or place the baby on their side. You can always put a rolled-up blanket behind their back to stop them from rolling over.

2 Place one hand on the back of the head and the other hand on the back. If the baby is on their side your hand will point either up or down the back, depending on what side you are sitting on.

Alternative energy balance

This alternative position for balancing a baby's energy focuses more on the stomach area and the back of the heart, so it is useful when they have tummy upsets or wind and will help to make a child feel safe.

1 Whether the child is on their back or stomach, or sat up, place one hand on the stomach and another on the back. In this case, it will be easier to place your hands in a horizontal position. This will balance energy throughout the body and calm the digestive system.

Treating the elderly

Elderly people are increasingly isolated in many societies. Many live out their later years without a partner and without the benefit of family living nearby. Even if they have people to talk to, the one thing they are all too often missing out on is touch. This lack of physical contact contributes to physical decline and also makes it more difficult for them to recover from illness. This is why a pet can be so important to an older person; stroking an animal goes a long way to replace human touch.

Older people also grew up in an era when people were more inhibited about their bodies. The idea of removing their clothes for a massage does not appeal at all to an elderly person, and although they would benefit from this type of therapy there is a psychological barrier preventing them from accepting it. For these reasons, Reiki is the perfect treatment for the elderly, as are reflexology, Indian head massage and acupuncture, because none of them are as intrusive as massage, but still provide touch as a key element.

Common conditions

The elderly are likely to suffer from chronic conditions such as arthritis, and Reiki can be very beneficial for alleviating the pain experienced in the joints. It is also useful for treating the sleeping problems that are common among this age group. Older people are also more likely to have long spells in hospital, and you can offer them Reiki to strengthen them before an operation and to speed recovery afterwards.

It can of course be used to treat terminal conditions, and although there can be no guarantee of remission at any age Reiki can gently guide a person through the end-of-life journey and help them reach a peaceful transition.

Dealing with mobility problems

Giving Reiki treatments to an elderly person is no different to treating any other adult. However, you may have to take their physical mobility into consideration. It may not be possible for them to get onto a treatment table. If this is the case, treat them in a sitting position on a straight-backed chair. When you want to treat their back, ask them to sit sideways on the chair.

An alternative with the elderly is to use distance healing. This allows them to relax in bed or on the sofa without worrying about their mobility.

RIGHT The elderly often miss out on the health benefits of touch, which makes Reiki, reflexology and Indian head massage ideal ways of compensating for this.

Reiki before and after surgery

While the elderly are hospitalized more frequently than other age groups, the need for an operation can happen to people of any age. Medical techniques have advanced to the point where many conditions are now treated by day surgery, using only a local anaesthetic. However, other conditions can only be treated with major surgery, which requires a general anaesthetic and a hospital stay afterwards. All surgery is invasive at all levels of the body, and when combined with anaesthetic severely weakens the body.

Pre-operative treatment

For some people, surgery has to be delayed because the surgeon considers that their body is not strong enough to undergo the operation. If this is the case, give the person as many full body treatments as possible to strengthen them. You may also want to concentrate on the area of the body that is to be operated on. If you cannot be with the person, sending distance healing to them for several days before they are due for surgery is just as effective – I have treated many people before surgery using this method.

LEFT Reiki can strengthen the body and mind before surgery, and support the post-operative healing process.

Even if there are no problems with the person being ready physically for surgery, many people, especially children, are apprehensive about the procedure. Reiki treatments will help them to deal with their fears and approach the operation in a more relaxed way.

Post-operative treatment

Once the operation is over, Reiki can be used to aid a faster recovery. One of the many advantages of Reiki is that you don't need to apply any pressure to the body; indeed, you don't even need to touch the body at all. Therefore, you can give Reiki without any fear of hurting the recipient. It may not be possible to give a full treatment while the person is still in hospital, but you can give a localized treatment to the wound area, holding your hand just above it for five minutes or more. You can supplement this by giving a full body treatment using the distance method.

Distance healing means that you can also treat people in intensive care, babies in incubators and those needing to be kept in isolation. With Reiki, distance or hospital visiting times and any other limitations need not prevent you from supporting anyone during a time that is stressful and often traumatic, allowing you to feel part of the healing process.

Treating animals

Pets are a valued part of the family, and it can be very distressing when they are injured or ill. Reiki can be used to complement medical treatment and support the pet's recovery in exactly the same way as for any other family member. When animals are ill, they are more instinctive about how to help themselves than humans. They stop eating to rest their system, for example, and they sleep to conserve energy.

The procedure for treating animals is not very different to that for treating humans. Anatomically, most animals' organs are in a similar position to human ones, so it will be simple enough for you to cover all the major ones. Obviously, animals present some challenges in that you cannot communicate with them verbally; therefore you will have to rely more on your skills of observation and your intuition. Some animals are more receptive to Reiki than others. This is down to individual character rather than breed. If a pet doesn't want to receive Reiki, don't try to hold them down and force it on them. It is better to let them walk away, and maybe try at another time.

Cats and dogs

When treating a cat or dog, you will have to place your hands in whatever positions you can comfortably reach. If possible, I start by placing my hands behind the ears, as this seems to calm the animal. If they are happy to sit still, I then work my hands down both sides of the body, and also put one hand on the chest and another on the back. Don't be concerned if you cannot work your way round the entire body, as the Reiki will flow right through it. If the animal has a wound, avoid touching it directly and work with your hands off the body. The time you spend on a treatment depends on the size of the animal and the length of time it decides it will stay still.

Other animals

'Exotic' pets, such as snakes and iguanas, that are used to being handled can be treated in exactly the same way. Birds may present problems, as they may not like being held. In this case, direct Reiki through the cage to them. In a similar way, fish can be treated by placing your hands on the tank. Horses will usually be quite receptive to having hands-on treatment, as they are used to being handled.

RIGHT Treating animals is not dissimilar to treating humans, although you will find that some animals are more receptive to Reiki than others.

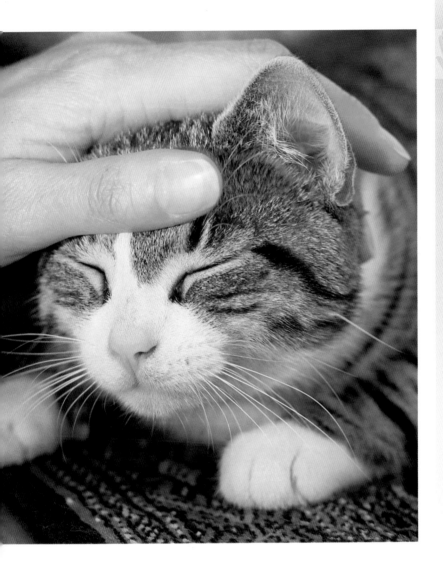

Treating plants

Life energy is as much an intrinsic part of vegetation as it is of animals and humans. Therefore Reiki can be used in a number of ways to enhance the life of all your plants.

Indoor plants

Begin by giving Reiki to the roots of the plant, by placing your hands around the pot. This is important because the roots are where the plant takes in the sustenance it needs to survive. When you feel intuitively that the roots have taken in enough energy, move your hands up to the body of the plant. Holding your hands about 2.5 cm (1 in) away from the leaves, allow the Reiki to flow through the aura of the plant.

Of course, even with Reiki your plants will need to be looked after in the normal way. Reiki will not help if the plant needs to be repotted. If a houseplant is not thriving, despite your best efforts, it may be an indication of negative energy in the spot where you have placed it. Plants are good indicators of energy black spots, so try moving it to another part of the room, or to another room altogether, and see if it starts to flourish again.

Garden plants

If you are putting in bedding plants, give Reiki to the roots before planting them. Bedding plants usually come in small pots, so simply hold the pot in your hands. If you are growing flowers or vegetables from seed, you can either give Reiki to the seeds in the packet, or you can hold your hands over seed-trays. This is an ideal opportunity to experiment with the effects of Reiki, as you could give Reiki to just half the seeds or seedlings, and then compare their growth rate.

If you have a very large garden, it is probably impractical to try giving Reiki to everything in it. Instead, you could use the distance healing method to give Reiki to the entire garden.

If the weather permits you can do this sitting in the garden, visualizing it in your mind and drawing the symbols on your hands as described on page 175, or, if it is too cold or wet, you can send the healing from the warmth of indoors.

LEFT Plants are known to respond well to the human voice giving them encouragement to grow, and also react well to being given Reiki.

PART 6
Reiki for life stages

Life and longevity

One of the main concerns of many people is the ageing process. Indeed, this concern seems to be starting at an earlier age than ever with people in their 30s complaining that they are old already. We seem to fear getting older, yet we also want to live longer, and we can expect to enjoy longer lives than previous generations. We want longevity but we don't have the means to enjoy it, and instead the majority stumble along to the end of life feeling defeated by their own body.

A slow decline

The real problems of ageing are not the dramatic events such as heart attacks, but the slow decline in body functions that start for some in the mid-30s and become more apparent after 60. Failing eyesight, impaired hearing, loss of mobility and memory, insomnia and dizziness are more defining of the problems of age than sudden events, such as strokes. It is the things that creep up on us quietly that depress us.

The prevailing message of the media and of orthodox medicine is that experiencing the problems associated with ageing is inevitable. People expect to lose mobility and develop chronic conditions, and in the West we have no clear idea of how to prevent or slow down physical or mental decline.

How Reiki can combat ageing

Reiki offers a way with which we can slow down this decline and, when taught to the already elderly, empower them again. Reiki cannot change your chronological age, but it can alter your functional age. Studies in China of men and women over 60 who practise Chi Kung have shown that many of them have the health and vitality of a person half their age. In this case, it is the combination of working with Ki and gentle movement that promotes longevity. As one Chi Kung teacher pointed out, however, longevity is only desirable if it increases the period of youthfulness, not that of old age.

Reiki, used through all the life stages, will increase our vitality as we draw in and balance the Ki needed to keep our bodies in optimum condition. It will give us a more positive outlook on life, and this in itself is one of the most potent methods of combating ageing. The perception that when we reach a certain age we no longer have a contribution to make to society is one of the major causes of physical and mental decline. Reiki gives us the wisdom to know better.

RIGHT Reiki may not be able to alter your chronological age but it can alter your functional age to that of a younger person.

Change and transition

During our lives we will face some major changes. We anticipate our teenage years with excitement, and then spend three or four years in a battle with our hormones while trying to establish a sense of self that causes our moods to alternate between depression and elation. We then face the responsibility of adulthood, and often the transition from being single to being in a relationship. This may be followed by one of the biggest changes in our lives – becoming a parent.

While parenting does not have an end point, we have to face the fact that our children will leave home. For many, this is another change that presents them with emotional challenges, including the loss of a sense of purpose for their lives. For women, this loss is often swiftly followed by another major life change – the menopause – dealing them a 'double whammy' within a short space of time. Not only are they no longer required to be a mother on a daily basis, but they also see themselves as being redundant as women.

The final challenge we face is the death of loved ones and our own approaching end of life. This change must also be faced by our children, for whom the death of a parent is also a life change.

Turning fear into wisdom

If we are balanced in our body, mind and spirit, we can move through these changes and transitions with more ease and serenity. We will have the wisdom to value change rather than fear it. Fear cripples us and prevents us from accessing our inner power to transform situations and find solutions to problems based on our inner wisdom. Often it is our inability to live in the present that allows fear to control us.

Reiki offers us the possibility of transforming our fear. By practising Reiki regularly we can approach any change in our circumstances with more flexibility and positivity. Reiki teaches us not to resist those experiences we would rather not have, but to flow with them, and observe them as lessons. We must not deny the pain and suffering certain events cause us, just as we should never deny ourselves feelings of joy. It is all part of the whole.

Reiki also teaches us that experiences of any kind don't last forever, and that the only permanent thing in our lives is the Light within us. When we are conscious of this, we can face anything.

LEFT Our lives are filled with constant change. We can help ourselves to move fearlessly through the many transitions we face by practising Reiki.

Adolescence

The adolescent years are a roller-coaster ride during which at best we celebrate the fact that we are almost independent, and at worst we fear that independence and what it will bring us. It is a period of transition that sees our personal interests change radically as we try to establish a personal identity. We look to clothes, music, sports and other activities to help us do that.

It is also a time when we struggle with our body image. If we lack confidence about the way we look, this can lead to social isolation or more serious disorders. Our body appears to be out of control,

and so do our emotions. Adolescent emotions swiftly change from one extreme to another, which can be frightening, as there seems to be no sign of a middle way.

Reiki can help teenagers through the ups and downs of this transition period by increasing their feeling of security and trust in themselves. As well as helping mental states such as mood swings, which are also partly hormonal, it is also a very useful aid with some of the more physical aspects such as acne and period pains. Whether you give Reiki to a teenager, or teach them Reiki so that they can self-treat, Reiki will support them through this period of uncertainty into adulthood.

With religion generally out of fashion, many of today's teenagers have no reference point at all for the benefits of spiritual values and practices. Although teenagers like to appear 'cool' and more mature than they actually are, they also have a yearning to feel some solidity and structure in their life that a spiritual practice could provide them with. I have found that most teenagers I meet are intrigued by Reiki and, most importantly, they see it as being 'cool'.

LEFT As teenagers, we struggle with our body image and try to establish our own identity. Reiki can help increase feeings of security and balance mood swings

Balancing the emotions

This treatment will help the recipient to release emotions and relax. The hand positions focus on the nervous system and the adrenal glands, which helps to strengthen the nerves and prompts the parasympathetic nervous system to kick in (see pages 120–121). Positions one to seven below calm the mind.

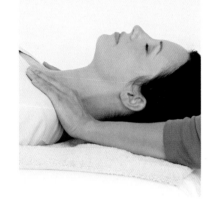

1 Place your hands in position 1a (see page 221).

2 Place your hands in position 1b (see page 221).

3 Place your hands in position 2a (see page 222).

4 Place your hands in position 2b
(see page 222).

5 Place your hands in position 3a
(see page 223).

6 Place your hands in position 3b
(see page 224).

7 Place your hands in position 3c
(see page 224).

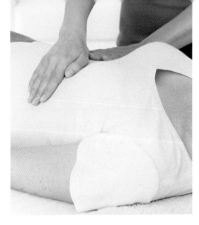

8 Place your hands over the heart chakra, covering the thymus gland to help to connect with the heart.

9 Place your hands in position 6 (see page 228).

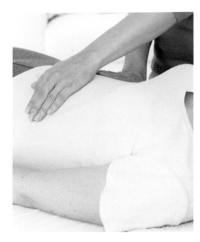

10 Place your hands in position 7 (see page 229).

11 Place your hands in position 14 (see page 236).

Pregnancy

Pregnancy is a momentous time in any woman's life. She is full of joy at the prospect of bringing forth a new life, but also filled with fear for the baby growing inside. Mothers-to-be have a lot to cope with during pregnancy, including all the body changes that take place, such as morning sickness, excessive tiredness, indigestion and backache, all of which can cause a lot of discomfort. These can all be alleviated with the use of Reiki.

Reiki can also support the woman emotionally during this time of upheaval.

Giving a Reiki treatment is also a way for fathers-to-be to become more involved with the pregnancy, and to help them bond with the unborn child in a different way. This may also help the father overcome some of the emotional challenges he faces in the months before the birth. Like the mother, he must face the responsibility of being a parent, and he must also come to terms with the fact that his relationship with his partner will change to some degree, as they both make room in it for a child.

Treatments during pregnancy and labour

Throughout the pregnancy, the mother should give a self-treatment every day. Reiki is not harmful at any stage and can be used to maintain calm and relaxation at all times. If the mother is not practising Reiki herself, then receiving treatments regularly from a practitioner will be beneficial. She should ask the practitioner to focus on any areas of particular discomfort.

In later pregnancy, it may be difficult for the woman to get comfortable on a treatment table, or even to get on or off one. In this case, treat her on a chair and limit the treatment time. Give Reiki directly to the areas where you can feel the baby moving. This will help the baby to absorb the energy directly. The baby will probably move towards the energy.

Give distance treatments to pregnant women during pregnancy, and particularly during the birthing process. It is enormously helpful, as the following case study demonstrates. In an ideal world, it would be great to have a Reiki practitioner (preferably the father) with the mother throughout labour. Failing this, a group of Reiki practitioner friends could take it in turns to send distance treatments. Involving several people in sending Reiki will increase the intensity of the energy, but one practitioner is enough to make a difference.

RIGHT Reiki provides a mother with support through both physical and emotional changes during pregnancy and can help both parents to bond with the baby.

Case study: giving birth with Reiki

My friend Anne was expecting her first baby. I mentioned the fact that Reiki treatments would be very beneficial to her and the baby but, as we were both very busy with work and lived some distance from each other, we never managed to find the time for any treatments.

Suddenly, there were only a few weeks to go before the baby was due. Up until this point, Anne's pregnancy had progressed well. However, a routine scan showed that the baby was underweight for the due date, and Anne was ordered to rest in bed for at least a week. She was, of course, very upset about this.

While she was stuck in bed, I was a long way away. I then realized that the best thing I could do was send her Reiki by distance healing. She agreed to this and I sent her several treatments during the week she was resting. The next scan showed that the baby had put on some weight, but on the advice of their gynaecologist Anne and her husband decided to proceed with an elective Caesarean.

I sent Reiki to Anne the night before she went into hospital, and then again about half an hour before she went into the operating theatre. A short time later, her husband called to say they had a lovely son, who turned out not to be underweight at all. I visited Anne the next day and gave her Reiki for about ten minutes over the site of the incision, without touching it. For the next few days I sent her Reiki, visualizing giving her a full treatment but focusing on the lower abdomen. When she returned home, her health visitor was amazed to find that the scar had almost healed. Anne also recovered much faster from the Caesarean than anyone else I have ever come across.

This story shows that Reiki can be used with any situation that may arise during pregnancy and birth, and that it can be combined with orthodox medical procedures.

The menopause

The arrival of the menopause indicates a life change on several levels. In general, it occurs sometime between the mid-40s and early 50s, although it would appear that many women are now experiencing it earlier than in previous generations. This could be due to a number of factors, including diet and lifestyle.

In Western culture, the menopause is seen as an unwelcome event. This negative view of it, and of menopausal women, leads women to have a more unpleasant experience of some of the symptoms. By contrast, in cultures where menopause is seen as a positive event, women experience fewer problems with it and maintain a better self-image.

Orthodox medicine treats women with hormone replacement therapy (HRT) to compensate for the loss of oestrogen and progesterone that brings on the menopause. However, while this may reduce some of the symptoms, it also has its own risks and is not suitable for everyone. Alternatively, many herbal remedies are available that when combined with a diet rich in soya-based foods act to reduce the typical symptoms of night sweats, hot flushes, mood swings, vaginal dryness and loss of memory.

Our attitude to the changes taking place and the symptoms contribute a great deal to the ease, or lack of it, with which women go through the menopause. It is difficult for many women to have positive feelings about the menopause when they live in a culture that sees menstruation as 'disgusting' and 'unclean'. Our conditioning with regard to our menstrual cycle, makes it very unlikely that we can move through the menopause with ease, even though, ironically, it means the end of something we are taught to see as a problem.

Reiki can help women to cope with both the physical and emotional aspects of the menopause. It can help us to see this turning point in our lives as an opportunity to revisit our attitude to life. We can use it to clear out the old habits that no longer serve us as we enter this new phase, and replace them with a new strength and self-awareness that will enable us to see this event as full of possibilities, rather than as the end of them.

Weight gain

During the menopause, the metabolism slows down, resulting in unwanted weight gain. This position will help to control this.

1 Place one hand lightly over the throat area and one hand on the crown of the head. This position covers the thyroid gland, which maintains metabolism.

1

Hot flushes and sleep problems

The pituitary and pineal glands control the endocrine system; therefore it makes sense to treat the head area to alleviate symptoms that arise from an overall hormone imbalance.

1 Place your hands in Position 1.

2 Lay your hands horizontally over the crown of the head, with your lower hand just curving over the back of the head.

1

A *Ki* exercise for the menopause

This Chi Kung exercise will help to regulate your hormone levels. It is also an effective exercise for the prevention of osteoporosis, associated with the menopause. Keep your arms rounded and relaxed throughout the exercise. Repeat the exercise 4–6 times initially, and gradually build up to 12, 24 or 36 times. As you become more proficient with this exercise, you can build up a faster rhythm, and if you wish you can do it to music with a suitable beat.

1 Begin in a standing position with your knees slightly bent, your spine straight and your arms relaxed by your sides.

2 Slowly raise your hands to bring them above your head, your palms facing the sky. As you bring your hands up, rise onto the balls of your feet. Continue raising your hands until they are above your head, and keep stretching upwards.

1

2

3 Once your hands are right up above your head, turn your palms around so that when you come to lower them they will be facing the earth. Maintain your balance by keeping your eyes open, but relaxed throughout.

4 Swing your hands back down to your sides as you bounce down onto your heels. Allow the downward movement of your arms to complete a full, natural swing. Once you are in a rhythm, the energy will draw your arms back up.

Death and bereavement

Dying is the final transition we make. It is also the one we fear the most and the one that we cannot, for the most part, calmly contemplate. The quest for eternal life is embedded deeply in the stories of our culture, yet all of them conclude that death cannot be cheated. We may have the means to extend life, but we cannot live for ever.

To lose our fear of death is to find freedom. When death is accepted as just another part of the journey, it liberates us from our fear of living. All spiritual traditions teach that we will not cease to be, but will simply be transformed. Yet we have an attachment to our physical bodies that limits our thinking, and even those with deep belief find it difficult to connect to these teachings absolutely, because there is no proof. We don't have proof of other things, but that is of less concern to us than being certain about what happens after death.

Because Reiki works on all levels it can help a person approach the transition of the soul from the body in a way that helps them see it within the context of their whole life. In the same way, it can support us through the grief that follows a bereavement, and help us to understand that only the physical body has gone – the soul of the person still exists and may be communicated with.

When we treat the dying with Reiki, we should not confuse healing with curing. Although the possibility of a miracle is always there, it is perhaps more helpful for the Reiki practitioner to see Reiki as a means to help people through their death rather than as a way to keep them alive.

LEFT Reiki works to help a person make the transition from this life to that which lies beyond with less fear.

Case study: being reunited through Reiki

I remember on one occasion giving a talk about Reiki at an exhibition. Towards the end of the session, I decided to do a visualization with the audience. The purpose of this was to create a healing sanctuary of Light within, which could be visited whenever necessary. Afterwards I was approached by a man who came to thank me for the talk and especially for the visualization, because during it he had seen his wife for the first time since she died and had been able to converse with her. I am glad that I chose that exercise that day, and that he was there to experience it. Of course, it was no coincidence.

PART 7
Reiki for health and well-being

Food and energy

Food contains life energy, and is one of the most important ways we have of taking energy into our bodies. We then utilize this energy through the metabolic process. Therefore, when we eat food of a higher quality, the energy that we can take from it is also much better.

Foods that have a better quality of energy to begin with are organically grown or farmed foods, fresh produce (even if not organic) and foods eaten raw. Raw foods contain the most life force, as no cooking process has altered the nutrients in any way. Indeed, raw-food diets have become very popular, but this regime does not appeal to the majority of people who want a variety of hot and cold foods.

The food with the least energy is processed food. Even frozen vegetables are preferable to the canned variety. However, pre-packed and processed foods are very much a part of Western diets, owing to their convenience, and for some people their lower cost is another factor.

Giving Reiki to your food

Reiki can be used to improve the quality of all your foods, even a sticky toffee pudding. You can give Reiki to your food while cooking it by holding your hands above the saucepan but take care that you don't get burned by steam or splashed by oil. Perhaps a safer alternative is to give Reiki to your food when it is on the plate. At home, you can hold your hands above the plate. In a restaurant, you can also give Reiki to a meal by discreetly placing your hands on either side of the plate, with your palms facing in.

Any beverage can also be treated with Reiki. Coffee and tea can be treated before it is made, and children's squashes and juices can also be treated in their containers. Even water and wine can be improved with Reiki.

The joy of juice

Juicers have made it easier for us all to consume more fruits and vegetables without having to crunch our way through a bag of raw carrots every day. They are also a wonderful way to get children to eat more vegetables – combining vegetables such as celery and carrots with fruits such as apples, oranges and pears is more appealing to their taste buds.

RIGHT Reiki can be used to remove toxins from our food and add energy to it, which will benefit our bodies.

Food and the chakras

Food can also be used to balance the chakras. A chakra therapist will be able to advise you on the correct foods to include in your diet, and those you should exclude. You can, of course, apply some of the principles to your diet yourself, but if you have a serious condition the therapy will be more effective if you consult an expert.

Research suggests that the elements in our food that give it colour, such as the beta-carotene that makes carrots orange, play an important role in balancing us. It has also been discovered that food when digested creates a vibrational energy based on colour light signals. These are absorbed by our cells via the bloodstream. Therefore,

in order to experience optimum health, we need to consume fresh foods the natural colours of which reflect the colours of the chakras. If a chakra is overactive, you should eat foods of the opposite colour to calm it; if it is sluggish and needs activating, eat a food of the same colour as the chakra.

As you can see from the chart opposite an underactive base chakra can be helped by eating red foods such as red peppers. However, if this chakra is overactive you should avoid red foods, especially hot foods like chillies. This applies to most of the chakras. Where a colour supports it if it is underactive, refrain from those types of foods if you feel that this chakra needs to be slowed down.

Introducing this concept into your diet, combined with giving Reiki to your food (see page 288), will help to support you at all levels, and you will notice the benefits of consuming a better quality of energy. It will also encourage you to listen to your body more and to interpret what it is telling you more accurately. As a result you should feel more 'Oneness' with your own body, which will in turn create a sense of harmony with the rest of the Universe.

LEFT Eating foods of a certain colour can help to balance an underactive chakra of the same colour.

CHAKRA	COLOUR	FOODS
Base	Red	An underactive base chakra can be balanced by eating red fruits and vegetables, such as red peppers.
Sacral	Orange	Oranges, carrots and other orange foods such as pumpkins, peaches and sweet potatoes support this chakra.
Solar plexus	Yellow	Yellow citrus fruits stimulate physical and emotional release from this chakra. Bananas in moderation will also calm it.
Heart	Green	Salad vegetables and greens such as cabbage and spinach have a cleansing and balancing effect on the entire body.
Throat		
Brow /Third eye	Blue and purple	Blue or purple foods such as blueberries and aubergines are connected to balancing our mental and spiritual levels.
Crown		

Dealing with stress

Stress is increasingly becoming the root cause of many illnesses. More and more people are attending doctors' surgeries with a variety of symptoms that medics now diagnose as being stress-related. Until recently, stress was not acknowledged by the medical profession as a legitimate source of disease, but the evidence of studies in recent decades has reversed this thinking.

Although we have more leisure time than our ancestors, and an array of gadgets to make mundane tasks easier, the technology that has made this possible has also brought with it a culture of multi-tasking. We are constantly under pressure at home and work to juggle several tasks simultaneously in order to maximize our use of time. Similarly, the use of mobile phones and email means that for many the working day does not end at 5 p.m. as it once did, as there is an expectation in many professions that employees will be available to resolve problems on an almost 24-hourly basis.

Many of us are not very good at recognizing that various symptoms we are experiencing are caused by stress, or that stress may at least play a part in them. We may even deny that we could be suffering from stress as we consider ourselves to be immune to it. A failure to consider the possibility that we are affected by it naturally leads to a recurrence of symptoms. Orthodox medicine may relieve the symptoms temporarily, but unless the underlying cause is dealt with, which is in all probability an emotional issue, then the condition reappears.

Despite the increase in stress-related illness, the majority of us are not very good at releasing stress. Our coping mechanisms for dealing with stress tend to include drinking, overeating and slumping in front of the television. Physical exercise is a better method for combating stress, but it is better to take up something like yoga or Tai Chi rather than a highly competitive or extreme sport that will keep the adrenalin running.

Reiki treatments are an excellent stress-reduction method. Not only will they relieve the symptoms of stress, such as mood swings, anger and anxiety, but they will work on the root cause and help us to find ways to prevent us building up stress in the first place.

Relieving a headache or migraine

One of the most commonly experienced symptoms of stress is a headache or migraine. The following treatment positions help to relieve the symptoms and promote calm and clear thinking. Give the treatment for about 15 minutes. This can also be used as a self-treatment.

1 While sitting or standing, place one hand over the forehead and another across the back of the head, at the point where the head and neck join.

2 Place your hands on either side of the head with your palms covering the temples and your fingers pointing upwards.

3 Place both your hands on the back of the head with the fingers pointing upwards.

Work

Our work life brings us stress, but it can also bring physical problems such as back pain and repetitive strain injury (RSI) from long hours in front of computers without proper breaks. The increasing use of technology has intensified the pace at which we are expected to work, and we struggle to keep up with the speed of our communications systems.

Organizational factors also contribute to stress and illness – these include work overload, career blocks and dysfunctional working relationships. This is something that the employer ultimately has control over, but it is evident that many businesses are demanding higher productivity. The result of this stress for many workers is a weakened immune system, resulting in various recurring illnesses, and a decline in the nervous system, which may lead to a nervous breakdown.

There are two simple things you can do to alleviate physical and mental problems at work: sitting correctly and taking a break.

Correct sitting posture

Every time you sit down at your desk, adjust your posture to ensure your spine is straight and your feet are flat on the floor. Placing your bottom towards the front of the chair will help you to keep this posture. Avoid sitting with your legs crossed for long periods.

Take a break

Whenever possible, switch your computer off completely, particularly if you are in the habit of eating lunch at your desk. The constant noise, screen glare and electromagnetic radiation are all irritants to our body systems.

LEFT Sitting in the posture illustrated keeps the spine straight yet relaxed and your feet flat on the floor.

1 **2** **3**

Neck and shoulder treatment

One of the major physical symptoms of work stress is pain and tension in the neck and shoulders. It is difficult to self-treat the shoulders, so if possible get somebody to give you this treatment.

1 Place one hand over the forehead and another across the base of the back of the head.

2 Place the hands on either side of the upper spine with your fingers curving over the shoulders.

3 Place one hand between the shoulder blades and the other in the centre of the chest, covering the thymus.

Family life

Living with other people is not always as enjoyable and straightforward as we might hope. Even the happiest families experience times of conflict. This is often a result of others not behaving as we want them to, and our tendency to project responsibility for imperfect situations onto other people. If these tendencies are not addressed, the result is a deterioration in a relationship that may ultimately result in the end of it.

Being less judgemental of others, and taking responsibility for events in our life that we don't like, will not only empower us but also improve all our relationships. Reiki has the potential to help us examine our likes and dislikes, our habits, our beliefs and the extent to which we are judgemental. Self-treatments and meditation on the spiritual principles will help you find a balance within, which will then be reflected in more harmonious relationships with others.

Self-treatment for anger

Spend at least 20 minutes on this treatment. This treatment focuses on areas of the body associated with anger: the throat, which we use to speak angry words; the head, where thoughts arise; the adrenals where we produce hormones that can fuel aggression and the heart, where anger may be resolved.

1 Place one hand over your forehead and the other across the lower back of the head.

2 Place your hands around your throat with the heels of your hands touching at the front and your fingertips curving round the back.

3 Then place your left hand over the kidney and adrenal area on your back and your right hand over the lower left side of the ribcage in the area of the spleen.

4 Place one hand in the middle of the chest, over the heart, and the other hand above it, covering the thymus gland.

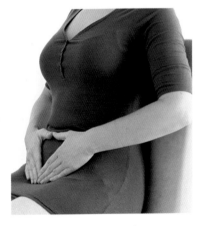

5 Place one hand on your solar plexus and the other below the navel, over the sacral chakra or *Hara* below the naval.

6 Finally, place your hands on your lower abdomen, making a V-shape, with your fingertips. Men could place their hands over the groin.

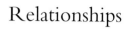

Relationships

One area of our personal relationships that most of us have a big problem with is intimacy. Many people are afraid to reveal their innermost thoughts to their partner because it makes them vulnerable. They fear being hurt or criticized through revealing their true selves. As a result, they defend themselves by remaining closed to the other person, unable to fully experience the support of an open, loving relationship.

Reiki can help by opening the heart chakra. When you experience this centre truly opening up, it brings a feeling of complete joy and peace.

Heart meditation

This meditation will help you open your heart and release the feelings within it.

1 Sit with your hands on the heart chakra giving Reiki to it, and visualize a rose-coloured energy entering it. Keep your hands in this position until you feel a sensation of softness in the area. You may find this very emotional. If tears come, let them flow. You may also want to contemplate everything and everyone around you while in this position, and meditate on feeling gratitude for it all.

Heart-to-heart meditation

This meditation will help you and your partner increase your feeling of intimacy.

1 Sit facing each other in a comfortable position, and close enough to touch each other's chests. Each of you should then place your right hand on your partner's heart chakra, and your left hand on your own heart. Keep the face and eye muscles relaxed as you gaze softly into each other's eyes for about a minute.

2 Staying in the same position, close your eyes and feel the Reiki flow through your hearts. You can stay in this position for as long as you like, although 15 minutes will probably be enough for you to connect with the heart energy and a experience a sense of union.

Connecting with yourself

All too frequently, we are so caught up with everything that is going on around us that we forget to give some time to ourselves and discover how we are feeling. Self-treating with Reiki is a wonderful way to spend some quality time with yourself and connect with how you are at all levels of your being. It will also balance and re-energize you.

Connecting exercise

Allow yourself at least 30 minutes for this treatment. If you can give yourself more time, do so. Try to make sure that the space you are treating yourself in also feels relaxed. It is difficult to relax amongst clutter as your mind tends wander towards clearing up even though your eyes are closed.

1 Lie on your back with your arms by your sides. Slow down your breathing and allow all your muscles to relax before beginning.

2 Place your hands over your eyes. Hold the position for five minutes.

3 Now place your hands over your heart and open yourself to feelings of love and gratitude.

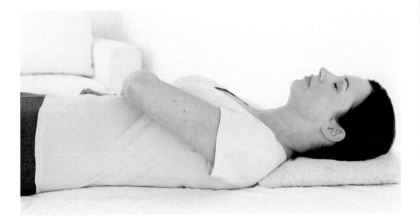

4 Place your hands adjacent to each other on the right side of your body, with one on your lower ribcage and the other beneath it on your waist. This helps to balance your emotions. Stay in this position and enjoy the sensation of being relaxed and taking care of yourself.

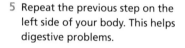

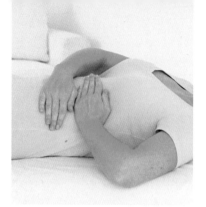

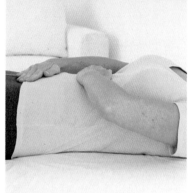

5 Repeat the previous step on the left side of your body. This helps digestive problems.

6 Place one hand on your navel and the other just below it. This position allows the energy to flow throughout your body.

7 Women should place a hand on each breast. Men should place both their hands in the middle of their chest. This helps both genders connect with their female energy.

8 Women should place their hands in a V-shape over the pubic bone, and men should place their hands in the groin area. This helps both genders to connect to their male energy.

9 Place your right hand over your forehead and your other hand just below your navel.

10 Place both your hands behind your head as if cradling it, with your fingertips facing upwards. This aids mental relaxation.

11 Finish off by allowing your arms to relax by your sides again, and take a few minutes to bring yourself back into an alert state.

Connecting with nature

Being surrounded by nature helps us to connect with the earth energy that is so important to us. You may notice that people who enjoy gardening, or activities such as hiking or surfing, often have the characteristics of being more relaxed, less nervous and more secure in themselves. This is because they are drawing in more grounding energy than people who tend to spend more time in mental activities.

Spending more time outdoors helps all of us to draw in more of the earth energy that assists us in understanding the essence of being human, and supports our creativity. Taking the opportunity to meditate in your garden, on a beach or in a park will strengthen your earth connection enormously.

Before I learned Reiki, or indeed knew anything about any alternative practices, I used to live next to a wood. One day I was pushing my son around the wood in his pram when I came across a group of people with their arms around the trees. I thought it was hysterically funny. After I learned Reiki and read lots of books on energy, I thought about those people and realized what they had been doing. I went to work at a hospital that had beautiful grounds with many mature trees, and the following exercise became one of my favourite ways of spending lunchtime, when the weather permitted.

Tree exercise

If you can bring the energy up on an in-breath and down on an out-breath it will add to the effectiveness of the exercise and help you harmonize with the tree's energy.

1 Standing or sitting, lean your back against a tree.

2 Feel the earth energy coming up through the roots and up the trunk to the tops of the branches. Visualize this at first, until you are able to sense it.

3 Now visualize the energy coming up through the soles of your feet and up through your body, through the crown of your head and up to the top of the tree.

4 Now bring the energy back down again through your body and into the earth.

PART 8
Reiki for common conditions

Reiki first aid

In general, Reiki has not been taught in the West as a method of treating specific conditions. Instead it is a treatment for all conditions, and the practitioner takes the same approach with every recipient, whatever problem they have. However, there has always been some acknowledgement in classes that Reiki can be used effectively when a person has an accident, and when a full Reiki treatment would not be possible.

Caution

This section of the book is not intended as a substitute for medical advice. While the advice and information are believed to be accurate and true, the reader should consult a physician in all matters relating to health and particularly in respect of any symptoms that may require diagnosis or medical attention. Reiki practitioners are not qualified to diagnose conditions, nor should they do so.

For example, if you have a headache it might be in your best interests to give yourself a full self-treatment, but it is not always necessary as you can just treat the head area. This applies to treating others for the same problem. Similarly, cuts, burns, bites and shock can be treated by focusing on the injured site immediately after the accident has happened.

This section looks at treatments for specific common conditions. These are not intended to replace full body treatments but to offer hand positions for focusing on the relevant areas of the body. Conditions such as anaemia, high blood pressure and others that are longer-term conditions and as such not strictly speaking 'first aid' are included here because self-treatment of specific points may help you when the condition appears to be worse than normal, or you have an acute flare-up. If you do have a chronic condition, regular, full body treatments are advised, but there may be times when you are not able to do this and simply want to ease the symptoms at work, when travelling or in other similar situations.

There are also some suggestions for each condition about the use of other complementary therapies that can be used alongside Reiki.

Case study: playing in the park

On one occasion I was in a local park with some other mothers and our children. One girl fell off a swing backwards and hit the back of her head. She was screaming with the shock of the accident as much as the pain, and while her mother gave her some arnica to help prevent shock and bruising I put my hand on the back of her head. To her astonishment, her daughter calmed down immediately. The mother was so impressed that she took a Reiki class soon afterwards. Indeed, children are likely to need first-aid Reiki for everyday accidents more often than adults, and it is a very useful addition to the first-aid box.

Shock

Shock causes a sudden reduction of the supply of blood to the vital organs, such as the heart, lungs and brain. Shock can be an emotional response to bad news or to seeing a highly disturbing event, or part of the response to a sudden accident, in which case there will be both a physical and a mental element. The body can also physically go into shock as a result of severe dehydration through diarrhoea. Symptoms include clammy and pale skin, shallow and rapid breathing, dizziness, anxiety, nausea, vomiting, coldness and shaking.

Physical shock is a part of some allergic reactions. For example, an allergic reaction, at its most extreme, makes people go into 'anaphylactic' shock. Most commonly, this is caused by eating nuts, and by bee or wasp stings. People who have this level of allergic reaction should carry anti-histamine in a hypodermic syringe with them at all times, as they need to be treated within minutes.

Reiki treatment

The symptoms of shock can appear frightening. Try to remain calm and in control as you give a treatment.

To bring a person out of a state of shock, place your hands on the solar plexus and heart areas. You can place both hands on the front at the same time, or on the back. Often it may be more comforting to treat front and back simultaneously. However, depending on the situation, you will have to adopt whatever position you can get to at the time.

Complementary treatments

- AROMATHERAPY OILS such as lavender, melissa or peppermint may be dropped on a handkerchief and held under the nose until the condition eases or until medical help arrives.

- BACH FLOWER REMEDIES Rescue Remedy is part of many first-aid boxes. You can either put 4 drops in 30 ml of water and drink it, or dab it on the temples and wrists to reduce symptoms.

High blood pressure

Blood pressure is the measurement of the force of the flow of blood through the arteries. When the pressure is abnormally high, it leads to a condition called hypertension. This condition increases the risk of heart attack and stroke. Hypertension is caused by a number of different factors, such as a family history of it, stress, alcohol consumption, smoking and diabetes, and it can occur during pregnancy. Symptoms include dizziness, headaches, fainting and visual disturbance.

It can also have emotional causes. When emotions – especially anger, frustration and grief – are repressed, they build up force internally, and if not released will threaten to explode at some point. Often when anger is expressed in this situation it is with such force that it drives the blood pressure up. This can be seen in reddening of the face.

Complementary treatments

- AROMATHERAPY OILS that have calming properties are helpful. Lavender is a good choice.

- BACH FLOWER REMEDIES Use remedies for the specific emotions being experienced.

- DIET Reduce intake of red meat, fats and salt.

- EXERCISE Non-competitive exercise, such as walking, swimming, yoga or Chi Kung, is excellent for lowering blood pressure naturally.

- MEDITATING on a regular basis, including visualizations that calm the mind, is beneficial.

Reiki treatment

The positions for treating high blood pressure are similar to those for treating anger as they may originate in similar areas of the body, such as the adrenals.

1 Place your hands over the thyroid area of the throat using Position 5. This will help emotional expression.

2 Treat the adrenals and kidneys using Position 14.

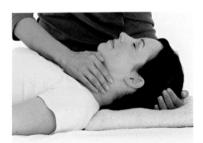

3 Place one hand across the back of the head and the other hand on the side of the neck to cover the major carotid artery.

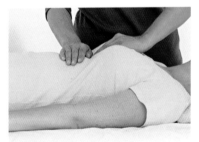

4 Place one hand on the heart and the other on the solar plexus.

Circulation problems

Problems with the circulation of blood around the body can be acquired, and in many cases people are born with what is usually referred to as 'poor circulation'. It is diagnosed as a condition in which the veins and arteries don't carry the blood around efficiently. Typical causes of this condition are hypertension, high cholesterol, excessive alcohol and smoking, as well as diabetes. In orthodox medicine, it tends to be treated by a combination of exercise, diet modification, and in some cases medication.

Emotional aspects of the condition may have roots in an unwillingness to be in the flow of life. For example, if you have poor circulation in your legs and feet, you may unconsciously not want to go in the direction your life is taking you.

Reiki treatment

Steps 1–3 can be used for self-treatment. Steps 4 and 5 can only be used on others.

1 Place your hands over the spleen, on the left side of the body, covering the lower ribcage and waist area, using Position 7.

Complementary treatments

- ACUPUNCTURE This is useful for stimulating the heart and spleen.

- DIET As with hypertension, circulatory problems benefit from a reduction in consumption of foods that are fatty and high in cholesterol.

- EXERCISE Walking and swimming are perfect activities for stimulating the circulation and detoxifying the system.

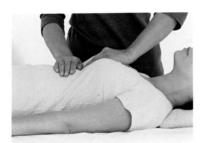

2 Then place your hands over the heart and solar plexus.

3 Place your hands in a V-shape on the tops of the legs with the fingers pointing away from you.

4 Place one hand on the shoulder and another on the wrist. Allow the energy to run up and down the arm. Repeat on the other side.

5 Finally, place one hand just below the buttock and the other on the sole of the foot, using Position 15. Repeat this on the other leg.

Anaemia

Anaemia occurs when the production and functioning of red blood cells is affected detrimentally. Red blood cells are produced in our bone marrow and are necessary for carrying oxygen around the blood. The most common form of anaemia is caused by iron deficiency. The other types of anaemia are aplastic anaemia, which is caused by very low production of red blood cells, and megablastic anaemia, which is caused by vitamin deficiency. Symptoms include fatigue, headache, dizziness and palpitations. Emotional aspects of the condition include unexpressed anger and fear.

Those most at risk of anaemia are the elderly, pregnant women and children with an unbalanced diet. Treatment is usually iron supplements and Vitamin B12, while more serious cases may require transfusions.

Complementary treatments

• AROMATHERAPY MASSAGE This (or any other therapy that increases feelings of self-worth and love) will help.

• DIET This is an important aid to treating this condition. The more iron you can take in naturally, the better. This is found in some fish, egg yolks and dark green, leafy vegetables such as spinach and broccoli. Foods rich in vitamins B12, C and E are essential for the absorption of iron. Avoid dairy products, caffeine drinks and tea, which interfere with iron absorption.

• EXERCISE Yoga or Chi Kung will improve liver function and general well-being.

Reiki treatment

The focus of a Reiki treatment for anaemia is on the liver, as this is the organ that metabolizes iron. The liver is a hard-working organ and deserves as much treatment as you can give it, as it is so important for many other functions of the body.

1 Treat the liver using Position 7.

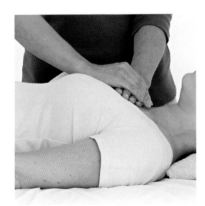

2 Then place your hands over the heart, also covering the area of the thymus gland.

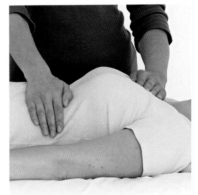

3 Place one hand over the thymus, and the other hand over the spleen. This helps to build the immune system and purify the blood.

Blood cholesterol

Cholesterol is a fat produced by the liver, or absorbed from foods that are high in cholesterol, such as dairy products. Cholesterol is used in the manufacture of hormones and is an important component of cells. However, although it is important, orthodox medicine states that a level of cholesterol above 160 mg/dl is dangerous for us, and that it is a leading cause of heart attack and stroke. Apart from our diet, diabetes and a hereditary disposition can raise cholesterol levels.

High cholesterol produces no symptoms; therefore the only way we have of knowing our level is to have it measured. It used to be the case that this required a visit to the doctor, but now testing kits can be bought at most chemists, so that you can monitor it yourself. Dietary changes are usually enough to reduce the level.

Emotional causes are a lack of joy in life and a very rigid way of thinking. Stress is also a cause of high cholesterol.

Complementary treatments

- DIET As mentioned above, this plays a crucial part. Including more wholegrains such as oats and barley will help, as will either eating plenty of garlic or taking a good garlic supplement.

- MASSAGE AND AROMATHERAPY MASSAGE These will reduce stress and treat the emotions.

- MEDITATION Meditating regularly to reduce stress will lower cholesterol levels.

Reiki treatment

These positions focus on organs associated with the digestive system and our metabolism of food. It is also aimed at improving our emotional attitude to life.

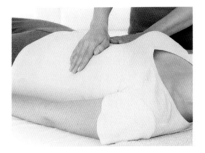

1 Place your hands across the upper ribcage using Position 6. This will treat the stomach.

2 Move your hands down one position to cover the liver, using Position 7.

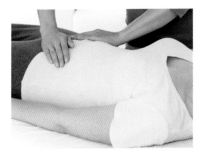

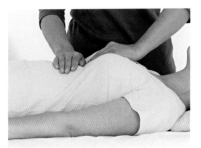

2 Move your hands down further to cover the spleen and colon, using Position 8.

4 Place your hands over the heart and solar plexus to increase a feeling of joy in life.

Diabetes

Diabetes is an increasingly common condition. Although it is very treatable, people need to be aware that this is a serious, sometimes life-threatening condition. It can also lead to a number of other serious conditions such as retinopathy, which can result in loss of eyesight. The fact that diabetics have increased in number points to some imbalance in the well-being of the general population, with diet and stress being the main culprits.

There are two types of diabetes. Type 1 is insulin-dependent diabetes, and arises when the pancreas produces little or no insulin. This type of diabetes is treated with daily shots of insulin and careful attention to diet and eating schedules. When a young person is diagnosed with diabetes, it is more likely to be this type. Type 2 diabetes occurs when the pancreas only produces a minimal amount of insulin. This type of diabetes can be treated with diet and exercise and tends to be caused by obesity and age.

Emotionally, people with diabetes may not be able to enjoy any sweetness in their lives, by giving love either to others or to themselves. They also have problems releasing stress, which is why the adrenals, liver and pancreas can become overworked.

Complementary treatments

- ACUPUNCTURE Treatment to support the liver and the adrenal glands will help.

- DIET Include more wholegrains and fruits, green vegetables, pulses and garlic. Avoid foods with animal fat, dairy products and sugar.

- EXERCISE Walk every day for 20–30 minutes, or attend a yoga or Chi Kung class every week – both offer exercises to strengthen the internal organs.

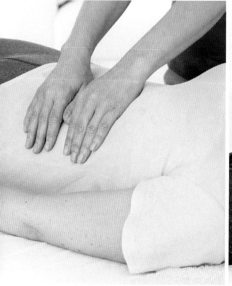

Reiki treatment

When there is no time for a full treatment, or it is impractical, these two positions will act as fist aid for the physical and emotional aspects of diabetes.

1 Treat the pancreas and liver with the hands placed one above the other as in alternative Position 6 and 7 (see page 299) but on the right side of the body.

2 Treat the adrenals and kidneys using Position 14.

Gallbladder disease

The gallbladder plays an important part in the digestive system, as it secretes enzymes and chemicals that enable us to digest our food. The most common symptom of problems with the gallbladder is the formation of gallstones, which cause enormous pain as they pass out of the gallbladder into the bile duct. The gallbladder may also become inflamed owing to the gallstones blocking the outlet.

Apart from the pain of gallstones, other symptoms of gallbladder disease are headaches, fevers and chills, along with irritability and being quick to lose your temper. Causes of the disease are a diet high in fats and cholesterol. Reducing these in the diet restores the gallbladder function and gallstones can dissolve naturally, although in some cases surgery is necessary to remove gallstones.

Emotional causes relate to the function of bile in the gallbladder. Bile has long been thought to represent bitterness and resentment. If you can learn forgiveness, you will reverse the negative emotions and their effects.

Complementary treatments

- ACUPRESSURE AND ACUPUNCTURE Both are helpful to stimulate the liver and gallbladder meridians.

- DIET Avoid meat, eggs, nuts and nut-based products, sugar, alcohol and dairy products. Increase your consumption of olive oil and juices such as apple, beetroot and carrot.

- EXERCISE Chi Kung offers exercises to strengthen the liver and gallbladder meridians, which you can do at home by yourself.

Reiki treatment

On the front of the body, work your way down from below the breastbone to the hip bone placing your hands across the body. This will probably take three steps.

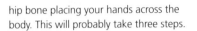

1 Treat the liver using Position 6.

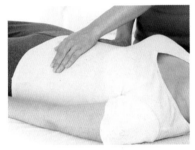

2 Move into Position 7 or alternatice position 6 to treat the spleen.

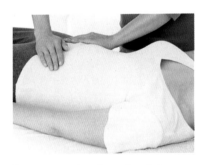

3 Place your hands on the abdomen in a V shape to treat the intestines, using Position 8.

4 Finally, treat the adrenals and kidneys using Position 14.

Toothache and gum disease

Toothache occurs at all ages. Most toothache is the result of tooth decay, inflammation of the pulp of the tooth, neuralgia or a dental abscess. It can also be caused by gingivitis, which affects the gums, or infected sinuses, in which case the person experiences what is known as referred pain.

The pain can be a continuous throbbing or intermittent, and may be caused by eating something that irritates the exposed nerve of the tooth. In many cases, it is caused by infection of the root nerve or the pulp. Tooth and gum disease is caused by poor dental hygiene and a diet that is high in sugar, fat and animal protein. A deeper-rooted emotional cause of the condition is thought to be an internal conflict over what we are saying to the outside world about ourselves. The teeth represent our foundations and feeling insecure may lead to problems with teeth and gums.

Severe toothache or an abscess on the tooth will usually require urgent dental treatment, but in all cases you can help relieve the symptoms with Reiki and some other treatments.

Complementary treatments

- ACUPUNCTURE Treatments to stimulate the liver meridian will help to relieve and prevent dental problems.

- AROMATHERAPY Tea tree oil, regularly massaged into the gums, will help to prevent infection.

- BACH FLOWER REMEDIES Rescue Remedy can be dabbed onto the infected tooth.

Reiki treatment

Toothache is one of the worst pains that we can experience. These positions alleviate acute pain, and the heat of your hands alone will feel soothing.

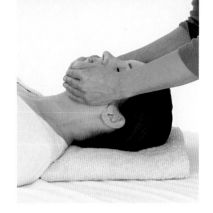

1 Cup the recipient's jaw in your hands with your thumbs tucked under the jawbone. This will treat the entire area.

2 Move your hands into Position 5. Remember that this position is different for self-treatment (see page 212).

3 Place your hands over the liver area on the right side of the body, using alternative Position 6 and 7 (see page 229).

Thyroid disorders

The thyroid gland regulates our metabolism and our levels of energy. Thyroid disorders come in two forms: hyperthyroidism and hypothyroidism. Each type produces different symptoms. A person with hyperthyroidism may experience weight loss, fatigue, anxiety, palpitations and sensitivity to heat. Someone with hypothyroidism will experience weight gain, tiredness, dry skin and sensitivity to cold.

Emotional causes may stem from a lack of commitment to the physical body. Those with hypothyroidism may also feel defeated and depressed by the process of living; those with hyperthyroidism have a stressed, nervous attitude to the issue.

Complementary treatments

- DIET Eat iodine-rich foods such as seaweed, raw vegetables, pulses and wholegrains.

- REBIRTHING This technique, using the breath, should be done with a trained therapist, but can be very helpful in clearing the emotions behind this condition.

Reiki treatment

These positions strengthen both the thyroid gland and the base chakra.

1 Treat the thyroid area using any hand position that feels comfortable to you. You can use Position 5.

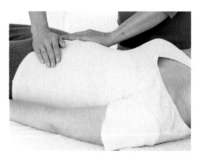

2 Treat the base chakra, using Position 8 or by placing your hands over the base chakra if you are self-treating.

Arthritis

Arthritis is an inflammation of the joints and has a number of forms. The four main ones are: **osteoarthritis**, which is a consequence of wear and tear on the joints and is both hereditary and age-related; **rheumatoid arthritis**, which is an auto-immune condition that primarily affects the hands, wrists and feet; **spondylitis**, an inflammation of the spinal vertebrae and pelvis; and **gout**, which occurs when there is a build-up of uric acid in the joints. Meditation, stretching exercises and heat treatment are the first line of treatment, with surgery used only in severe cases. If possible, give a full body treatment first.

Complementary treatments

- DIET Avoid dairy products, which build up calcium, and animal fats.

- EXERCISE Gentle stretching exercises performed daily will help to prevent stiffness.

- MEDITATION Meditate on letting go of rigid ideas and focus on the concept of being in the flow.

Reiki treatment

Focus on treating joint areas and getting energy to flow through the limbs.

1 Place your hands around the joint if possible. If not, place your hands side by side over the area.

2 Use Position 15 to run energy through the legs.

Burns and scalds, cuts and abrasions

Burns and scalds

The difference between burns and scalds is that burns are caused by forms of dry heat, such as fire, electricity, strong sunlight or chemicals, while scalds are caused by damp heat from boiling liquids and steam. The effects of both on the skin and soft tissues are the same, as is the treatment. With mild burns, the damage is restricted to the outer layer of the skin and symptoms include redness, pain, heat and sometimes blistering. Mild burns are seldom very dangerous unless they cover a large area of the body. With more serious burns, the damage goes deeper into the lower layers of the skin and produces blistering. The most serious burns affect the soft tissue and the nervous system and can be difficult to treat.

Immediate treatment for a burn is to bathe the area in cold water for 10–15 minutes, and then cover it lightly with a clean cloth or bandage. Don't put anything else on the site of the burn or scald, particularly not butter or fat. Furthermore, if material is stuck to the burn, don't try to remove it yourself. You should then seek medical treatment.

Cuts and abrasions

Most cuts and abrasions are minor and only the capillaries in the skin are damaged, causing a small amount of blood to be released into the surrounding tissues, or to escape the wound. This blood will soon clot if the cut is not deep, and requires little treatment. An abrasion is characterized by the upper layer of skin being scraped off, exposing the layer below.

There is less blood loss with an abrasion, but – as it is often caused by the skin being dragged along gravel or another hard surface – foreign particles may need to be removed from the area during the cleaning process. Cuts should be cleaned first, and pressure should be applied to the area to stem the flow of blood. If it is a hand that is cut, holding the hand upright helps the blood to flow away from the area. Both cuts and abrasions may need a light dressing to keep the area clean, but exposure to the air will help the healing process.

Cuts that are deeper, or are lacerated (meaning they are ragged and torn, such as those caused by glass), need medical attention, as stitches are probably required. If the wound is deep with a foreign body in it, it is better not to attempt to remove it yourself.

Complementary treatments

- BACH FLOWER REMEDIES
  Rescue Remedy should be given
  orally to alleviate stress and
  shock. Usually 4 drops in water is
  sufficient; it can also be used to
  clean the wound.

- HERBALISM Aloe vera gel may
  be applied to a minor burn or
  sunburn where the skin is
  unbroken. Calendula ointment
  will help healing after cleaning.

- SUPPLEMENTS Vitamin E oil
  may also be applied to minor
  burns after the area has been
  cleaned, as this prevents scarring.

Reiki treatment

It is important that you don't place
your hands on the wound itself,
but keep them above it. In the case
of a very light burn, Reiki may be
sufficient treatment combined with
the first-aid steps (page 328). With a
burn that looks more than superficial,
you should consult a doctor as soon
as possible, but can give Reiki while
waiting to see one. You can also use
the treatment for shock (page 310)
immediately after the accident has
happened if the person seems in
need of it. Reiki can help the
bleeding to stop very quickly.

1 Clean wounds before treatment.
  For burns, minor cuts and
  abrasions, treat by holding your
  hand over the affected area.

Eczema

Eczema is a form of dermatitis that frequently appears in infancy or may develop in older people. In children it is often linked to hereditary causes and a disposition towards allergies. For example, children who have eczema often also have asthma and/or hay fever.

The symptoms of eczema vary in their severity according to the individual, but are characterized by patches of skin that are inflamed, itchy and scaly. In the worst cases, the skin is often broken and bleeding from being scratched. It is usually treated with soothing creams and corticosteroids, although these are to be avoided for long-term use as they cause thinning of the skin. However, in some cases they offer the only relief. People with eczema usually need to avoid highly perfumed skin and bath products, and clothes made from wool and synthetic fabrics are an irritant to the condition.

Emotionally, eczema can indicate that we are irritated by something that we desperately need to release, such as a thought pattern, in order to allow it to be replaced by something new that we feel more comfortable with.

Complementary treatments

- OATMEAL BATHS Bathing in water that has had oatmeal added to it by placing the oats inside a muslin bag is very beneficial to eczema and other dry skin conditions. There are also skin and bath products containing oats that offer relief from the symptoms.

- HERBALISM Both Chinese and Western herbalists have a variety of plants that they use to detoxify the system and strengthen the liver and kidneys. Consult a herbalist to get the best product for you.

Reiki treatment

After carrying out steps 1 and 2, you may also want to treat localized parts of the body where there is an outbreak of eczema. When doing this, don't place your hands directly on the area but hold them above it.

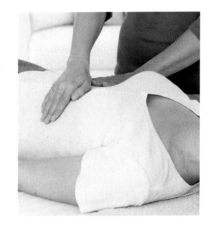

1 First treat the liver using Position 6.

2 Continue into Position 7 to further treat the liver.

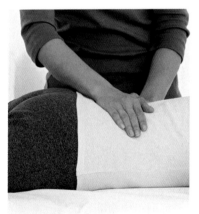

3 Treat the adrenals and the kidneys using Position 14.

Acne

Acne is an infection of the skin's sebaceous glands, which control the production of sebum, or oil, that keeps the skin from drying up.

The causes of acne are most likely a combination of hormonal overproduction and diet. Foods that make the blood overly acidic are probably responsible. These include dairy products, sugar and any foods high in fats, which are typically the main components of the foods that teenagers prefer.

The teenage years are ones of emotional upheaval and the fight for independence, so it is unsurprising that acne erupts as a reflection of this struggle to be our own person. As in other conditions that involve repressed anger, the liver is a focus for treatment when using Reiki for the condition.

Complementary treatments

• EXERCISE Any exercise that releases stress, such as swimming or dancing, is beneficial. Yoga and Chi Kung will also help, as they will quieten the mind and help to improve self-image.

Reiki treatment

Acne is helped by focusing on the head followed by the liver.

1 To tune into the recipient's energy flow, place your hands in Position 1a (see page 221).

2 Move your hands into Position 1b (see page 221), taking care to keep your touch light.

3 Place your hands in Position 2a or 2b (see page 222).

4 Place your hands in Position 3a (see page 223). Take as much of the weight of the head as you can.

5 Slide your hands into Position 3b (see page 224).

6 Hold your hands in Position 3c (see page 224), again taking as much weight as you can.

7 If you have Second Degree Reiki, draw Symbols 1 and 2, as in Position 4a (see page 226).

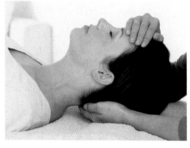

8 Place your hands in Position 4b (see page 225).

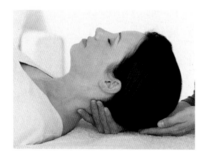

9 Use Position 4c (see page 226) to remove your hands gently from under the recipient's head.

10 Treat the throat by placing your hands in Position 5a (see page 227).

11 Pull your hands away in an arc, using Position 5b (see page 227).

12 Place your hands in the alternative Position 6 and 7 (see page 229).

13 Place your hands in Position 8 (see page 230). Remember the alternative position for men.

Insect bites

When an insect bites you, it pierces the skin to take in blood. Our bodies respond by producing an allergic reaction at the site of the bite. Usually this just causes some redness and swelling, but some individuals may have more extreme reactions, depending on the type of insect bite. Where a reaction is more unpleasant, the person may need to take anti-histamines; otherwise cleaning the site and using a cream designed to soothe insect bites will be sufficient. Mosquito bites in tropical countries may lead to malaria, which will need medical treatment, but in non-tropical areas mosquito bites don't cause a problem other than itching, and are more annoying than dangerous.

Although insect bites don't constitute a condition, if they overly bother you or you find them excessively itchy, it may be that they are reflecting an underlying emotion of irritation and frustration of which you are unaware.

Nettle stings and bee or wasp stings can be treated in much the same way as insect bites as they also produce an allergic reaction. This reaction indicates that the immune system could use a boost. The Reiki treatment opposite is aimed at supporting the immune system, as well as strengthening the liver and kidneys to help the body release toxins, which leads to the itching.

In the case of a small number of people, stings send them into anaphylactic shock. This is an extremely serious allergy with a fatal result if not treated immediately with an injection of anti-histamine. Giving regular Reiki treatments to a person with this extreme allergy will help to support them and may reduce the symptoms, but even so, it is important to remind them to always carry their anti-histamine.

Complementary treatments

- AROMATHERAPY Tea tree oil dabbed on the bite will help.

- BACH FLOWER REMEDIES Rescue remedy is helpful immediately after an insect has bitten you, or you have been stung. This is also available in a cream which can be applied to the skin. Impatiens also helps to release feelings of irritation.

Reiki treatment

The focus of this treatment is the liver and the kidneys to speed up the removal of toxins, and the thymus to strengthen the immune system.

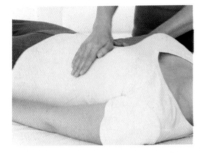

1 First, treat the liver area to release any toxins. You can use Position 6 (see page 228).

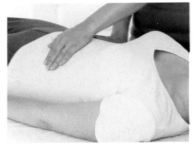

2 Continue into Position 7 (see page 229) , treating the right side of the recipient's body.

3 Treat the kidneys and adrenals using Position 14 (see page 236).

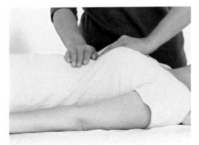

4 Treat the thymus, which is just above the heart, to stimulate the immune system.

Dandruff

Dandruff is defined as the shedding of skin primarily from the scalp, and is a form of dermatitis. People with other conditions such as eczema and psoriasis, and those with dry skin in general, are probably more prone to dandruff than others. It can also be brought on by stress, and by an allergic reaction to certain shampoos. Orthodox treatment is based on anti-dandruff shampoos, although severe cases may also require the use of corticosteroids and anti-fungal treatments.

Dandruff may also be the body's way of eliminating excessive amounts of proteins and fats in the diet, which the body is unable to digest. Other suggestions are that it might be caused by too much acidic food in the diet and by imbalances in the liver and kidneys. Emotionally, dandruff may indicate an excess amount of mental energy and the desire to shed old ideas.

Complementary treatments

- AROMATHERAPY Rosemary oil is wonderful for clearing dry scalp conditions. You can massage the scalp with a base oil to which you have added a few drops of the essential oil. If you don't want to make your own, you will find ready-made oils in health-food shops or places where they sell aromatherapy products.

- DIET Follow a diet with low-fat animal products such as white fish, raw vegetables, which you can take in juice form, and wholegrains.

Reiki treatment

The focus of the treatment is the body's elimination system: the liver and the kidneys. The adrenals are also treated to help reduce stress.

1 Place the heels of your palms on the crown of the head, fingers pointing down the side of the head.

2 Treat the adrenals and kidneys using Position 14 (see page 236).

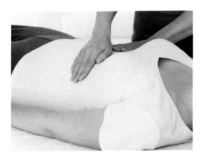

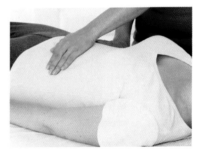

3 Place your hands over the liver area to support this organ using Position 6 (see page 228) or alternative Positions 6 and 7 (see page 229).

4 Continue treating the liver by moving into Position 7 or alternative Positions 6 and 7 (see page 229).

Allergies

An allergic reaction occurs when the immune system responds inappropriately to an otherwise harmless substance, such as grass. This reaction can be triggered by skin contact with perhaps a chemical or animal fur, by inhaling it (as with pollen), or by eating it (as in allergies to foods ranging from eggs and nuts to strawberries). Causes of the condition may be partially hereditary, and may be linked to other conditions such as asthma, or are the result of a weak liver and immune system, which is unable to fight the build-up of antigens (foreign substances) in the body.

Anti-histamines are used to treat some forms of allergy, such as hay fever. In severe cases, the person may need to be tested for the substances to which they are allergic, and undergo a course of desensitization treatments. With food allergies, the usual course of action is to eliminate various foods from the diet systematically, and observe the results. This usually requires consulting a nutritionist.

Emotionally, allergies are often made worse by stress of any kind. They may also be thought of as a refusal to accept personal power.

Reiki treatment

This treatment strengthens the immune system and the liver.

1 Place your hands on or over the face using Position 1 (see page 221).

Complementary treatments

- DIET Consult a nutritionist to adapt your diet to identify and then manage a food allergy.

- EXERCISE Some skin conditions can improve with regular yoga.

2 Move down to treat the throat area using Position 5 (see page 227).

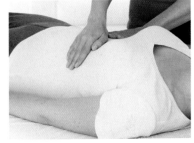

3 Place your hands horizontally below the breastbone, using Position 6 (see page 228).

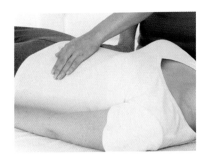

4 Move into either Position 7 (see page 229), and work your way down the front of the body to treat the lungs, liver and stomach.

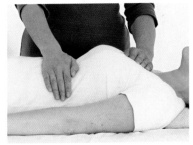

5 Place one hand on the thymus and the other hand on the spleen, which is in the area on the left lower ribcage.

Auto-immune disorders

Immunodeficiency or auto-immune disorders are a group of conditions characterized by the fact that the immune system fails to function normally, leaving the person susceptible to infections that a normal immune system would easily fight off. The conditions may either be congenital or acquired. For example, a person born with an immunodeficiency may find that they get recurring fungal infections. HIV is one example of acquired immunodeficiency through a viral infection; or the immune system may be suppressed due to use of certain medications. Many other conditions, such as lupus, rheumatoid arthritis, multiple sclerosis and diabetes, are also auto-immune disorders. There are no definitive medical answers as to the cause of immunodeficiency.

Emotionally, the condition could be brought on by trauma, stress and grief, all of which are known to leave even a healthy immune system somewhat weakened. As the thymus lies so close to the heart, the energy of the heart is closely associated with the condition, and it may indicate a lack of self-love and love from others.

Complementary treatments

- EXERCISE Take a yoga class, do light aerobic exercise such as walking, and find some balance in your life by setting aside time for recreational pursuits.

- HERBALISM Consult a herbalist about herbs that will strengthen the system and help particular related conditions.

- SUPPLEMENTS Vitamins B, C and E, as well as magnesium, selenium and zinc, will strengthen the immune system.

Reiki treatment

Stimulating the immune system is the first priority for a treatment followed by focusing on the areas responsible for removing infection from the body.

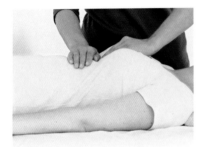

1 Place the hands over the thymus and the heart to stimulate the immune system.

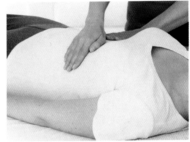

2 Treat the liver, spleen and pancreas on the front of the body. Start with Position 6 (see page 228).

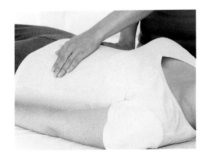

3 Move into Position 7 (see page 229), working down the body.

4 Treat the adrenals and kidneys with Position 14 (see page 236).

Back pain

Back pain comes in many forms and most people experience it at some point during their life. Happily, most episodes of it can be resolved with minimum treatment; however, chronic back conditions need either ongoing treatment or intensive treatment for intermittent flare-ups.

Chronic back pain has a number of causes: damage to the coccyx, pressure on the sciatic nerve, kidney infection, degeneration of the vertebrae and discs, and pain in the back muscles. Orthodox treatment usually includes painkillers and anti-inflammatory drugs, muscle relaxants and physiotherapy.

Emotional causes vary according to the area of the back affected. For example, lower back pain is associated with feeling a lack of material support and financial concerns. The middle back is associated with feelings of guilt and being unable to receive help from others, and the upper back and neck are connected with feelings of being burdened with responsibility for others and lacking emotional support.

Complementary treatments

- AROMATHERAPY Using oils such as camomile and eucalyptus put on hot compresses followed by cold compresses and held over the inflamed area will reduce pain and swelling.

- MASSAGE AND HYDROTHERAPY These are excellent ways to reduce inflammation.

- PILATES Consult a qualified Pilates instructor about specific exercises for your condition. Pilates has been very successful in helping many people with chronic back pain.

Reiki treatment

Treat the entire back, focusing on the area of most pain. This may mean adding some hand positions to cover the coccyx at the base of the spine, and also the sciatic nerve.

1 To treat the coccyx, place both hands over the tailbone. You can place your hands on top of one another, or place them side by side.

2 To treat the sciatic nerve, place both hands on the outer part of the right buttock. Repeat this on the outer part of the left buttock.

3 Use Position 15 (see page 237) on both legs to run the energy from the soles of the feet to the spine and back.

Sinusitis

The sinuses are pockets of air space around the nasal cavity. Sinusitis is a fairly common condition that is mostly an acute one, but in some people it becomes a chronic condition. Orthodox methods of treating it are with nasal decongestants, antibiotics and occasionally, if the condition is severe, by draining the sinuses surgically. Symptoms of sinusitis are pain around the nasal area and in the centre of the forehead along with the feeling of being unable to breathe properly.

Emotionally, we may be holding on to a deep mental conflict that we are unable to communicate to anyone, which results in us blocking it up and only releasing it drop by drop.

Reiki treatment

Focus on the sinuses to relieve congestion and on the liver to remove toxins.

1 Place your hands over the face, using Position 1b (see page 221).

Complementary treatments

- ACUPRESSURE AND ACUPUNCTURE These may help to clear blockages in the lymph system.

- DIET Remove all dairy products from your diet for a week. This will help to clear mucus from the system.

- AROMATHERAPY Inhaling oils such as eucalyptus in hot water will help to clear the nasal passages. You could also consider having aromatherapy massages to treat the emotional causes.

2 If you have Second Degree Reiki, draw Symbols 1 and 2 on the forehead. See Position 4a (page 225).

3 Place the hand you used to draw the symbols across the forehead. See Position 4b (page 226).

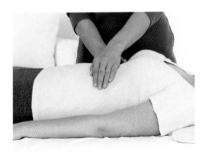

4 Treat the liver and spleen on the front of the body to help release toxic build-up. First use Position 6 (see page 228).

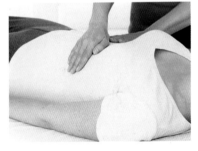

5 Continue into Position 7 or alternative Position 7 (see page 229), working down the body.

Menstrual problems

Menstruation relies on a combination of the development of the uterus lining and the regulation of hormone production. Problems arise when this delicate mechanism is not in balance. Problems manifest in different ways, the most common of which is dysmenorrhoea, usually called painful periods. The absence of menstruation, although normal during pregnancy, at other times is caused by anorexia and stress. The third type, menorrhagia, which is characterized by excessive bleeding, is usually caused by a hormone imbalance, intra-uterine devices and the presence of fibroids or polyps in the uterus.

Emotionally, menstrual problems point to a conflict with a woman's female nature. Symptoms tend to improve when a woman feels more comfortable with herself and her body.

Complementary treatments

• AROMATHERAPY Add a few drops of clary sage to the bath. However, it is probably better to consult an aromatherapist as some oils produce dramatic effects.

Reiki treatment

Treatments focus on the pelvic area and lower chakras.

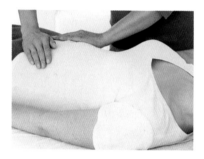

1 Treat the pelvic area, using Position 8 (see page 230). If self-treating, you may wish to treat the pubic area.

2 Treat the lower back by placing the hands in the centre of the back over the tailbone.

Prostate problems

The prostate gland is located at the opening of the urethra in men and is responsible for secreting the fluid that carries semen at the point of ejaculation. The prostate can become inflamed through bacterial infection, which is usually a sexually transmitted infection. This is treated with antibiotics. In older men, there is a tendency for the prostate to become enlarged. This causes blockages in the urethra and difficulties with urination. Surgery may be needed to rectify the problem.

Stress is a cause of the prostate problems, as is a diet that is high in animal protein and saturated fats. Emotionally, prostate problems may signal a feeling of impotence and frustration with sexual performance.

Complementary treatments

• MEDITATION This will help you to relieve stress and to accept the ageing process.

• YOGA A regular routine will relax the mind, and certain exercises strengthen the pelvic area.

Reiki treatment

Treat men for this as a matter of routine to prevent the condition.

1 With the recipient on his front, place one hand horizontally across the tailbone, and the other at a right angle to it, with the fingers pointing down the centre of the buttocks. You can also place one hand on top of the other to cover this same area.

Infertility

Infertility is the inability to conceive a child and may result from problems in either the male or female reproductive systems. Male infertility may be caused by blockages in the reproductive system, sexually transmitted diseases, genetic disorders, or low sperm count caused by stress, smoking and some drugs. Female infertility is typically caused by blocked fallopian tubes, the ovaries not releasing eggs, problems with the uterus that prevent implantation, and cervical mucus that destroys sperm.

Emotionally, couples with infertility problems may have issues with being in the present moment, and dwell too much on the past or future.

Reiki treatment

Treatment focuses on the reproductive organs and areas associated with stress.

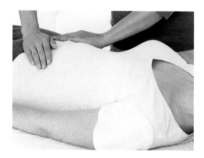

1 To treat the reproductive organs, use Position 8 for women (see page 230). For men, treat the groin area.

Complementary treatments

- DIET It is best to consult a nutritionist about following a diet that balances the body energy.

- EXERCISE Any exercise that decreases stress and promotes mental and physical balance is beneficial. Swimming, walking, yoga and Chi Kung are ideal.

2 Treat the adrenal glands and kidneys using Position 14 (see page 236).

Ear infections

Ear infections tend to be more prevalent among children, but adults may also experience them. Otitis media, an infection of the middle ear, is very common in children and is very painful for them. Other types of ear infection are: otitis externa, which happens in the ear canal; mastoiditis, in which pain is experienced in the bone behind the ear; and labyrinthitis, which is an infection of the inner ear. Earache can also be caused by referred pain from the teeth and jaw.

Emotionally, an ear infection may indicate that we don't like what we are hearing and want to block it out.

Complementary treatments

- DIET Remove dairy and wheat products, meat and sugar from the diet, and any foods known to be mucus-forming. Replace these foods with fruit and vegetable juices and plain foods such as steamed rice.

Reiki treatment

Treatment concentrates on the ears and their connection with the throat.

1 Place your hands over the ears with your palms covering the opening using Position 2a (see page 222).

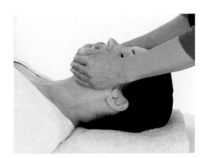

2 Then place your hands along the jawline, which will treat the connection between the ears and the throat.

Asthma

The number of people suffering from this condition, which is potentially life-threatening, continues to increase in many countries. It is caused by an inflammation of bronchi and bronchioles, resulting in constriction in the lungs, plus an increase in production of mucus, which narrows the airways. Symptoms include breathlessness, wheezing and coughing.

An attack can be triggered by allergens such as dust and pollen, by exercise and even by strong winds. Stress is another trigger, and girls and women may notice that their asthma gets worse for a few days before menstruation, indicating a hormonal link. Asthma usually develops in childhood and is often hereditary, but frequently clears up, or at least decreases in severity, once the adult years begin. However, it can suddenly develop in adults who have no previous experience of it.

Nutritionally, it is thought to be linked to an excess of dairy products and wheat in the diet. There is also a suggestion that it is more prevalent in children who are not breastfed or who are weaned too early. Emotionally, it is connected to 'overmothering', which leads to the child literally feeling smothered and unable to find space to be themself.

Please note that step 3 of this sequence is easy on men, but with women you will need to discuss if they are happy to have their breasts touched, or for you to hold your hands above them. Women can easily self-treat with this position.

Complementary treatments

- DIET Remove dairy and wheat products from the diet, and limit the amount of carbonated drinks children have, as these promote the production of mucus. Some food colourings may also exacerbate asthma.

- EXERCISE Learning the breathing techniques of either Chi Kung or yoga can help enormously with alleviating an attack or preventing its onset.

Reiki treatment

When treating someone during an attack it is preferable to prop them up with pillows on a sofa, or sit them on an upright chair.

1 Sitting behind the person, lay your hands below the throat in a V-shape with palms on the collarbone.

2 Place one hand on the thymus and another on the spleen, on the left side of the body.

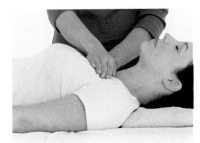

3 Place the hands horizontally across the upper chest. Keeping your hands in the same position, work down the entire chest area.

4 Move into Position 14 (see page 236). In Chinese medicine, weak kidney function is thought to cause asthma.

The common cold

There are very few people who have not had a cold at some time or other. Some people are particularly susceptible to colds and become infected several times a year. A cold is basically an infection of the linings of the nose and throat, and its familiar symptoms are nasal congestion, headache, sore throat, a runny nose and a cough. Colds are caused by viruses and treatment is according to the symptoms, which is why many households have an array of painkillers, nasal decongestants, cough medicines and throat lozenges in their cupboards. These, combined with rest and fluids to flush out the infection, are usually sufficient treatment.

Emotionally, a cold may be a sign that you need to slow down and take a rest.

Complementary treatments

• SUPPLEMENTS Increase your intake of Vitamin C and zinc while you have a cold, and ensure that these are part of your regular diet to prevent colds. Echinacea is also beneficial for both treatment and prevention.

Reiki treatment

Treatment focuses on the immune system, areas of infection and clearing toxins.

1 Place the hands over the face as in Position 1 (see page 221).

2 Then place your hands over or around the throat area using Position 5 (see page 227).

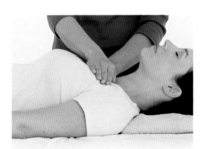

3 Place your hands horizontally across the upper chest. In self-treatments hands may be placed on the breasts.

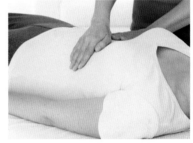

4 Treat the liver and spleen. Start with Position 6 (see page 228).

5 Move into Position 7 (see page 229) and work down the body.

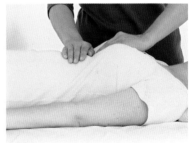

6 Place your hands over the thymus to strengthen the immune system.

Eye problems

There are many forms of eye problem, ranging from blindness at one extreme to simple eye strain at the other. In between there are astigmatism, strabismus (squint), short-sightedness and long-sightedness. These are all related to the refraction of light as it passes through the lens of the eye. For example, a short-sighted person can see objects close to them quite clearly, while anything in the distance is a blur. A long-sighted person experiences this in reverse. An astigmatism is the result of a malformed cornea, causing blurred images. A squint is caused by under- or overdeveloped eye muscles that alter normal vision. Eye strain is frequently experienced by those using computers for long periods of time without rest, and by those in professions that require focused reading of text and numerals.

The usual treatment for eye problems is to use glasses or contact lenses to correct vision. Laser treatment is also possible for more severe eyesight problems. Orthodox medicine does not recognize common eye problems that are unrelated to other conditions as having any root cause other than natural decline as part of the ageing process, or overuse of the eyes as part of work. Chinese medicine, on the other hand, indicates that a weakened liver function is responsible for decline in eyesight.

Emotionally, each type of eye problem has a different cause, but in general it is a refusal to see something. For example, a short-sighted person may only want to see what is in front of them, while a long-sighted person prefers not to see what is personal or close to them and spends their time looking into the future.

Complementary treatments

- ACUPUNCTURE This will stimulate the liver.

- EXERCISE There are several Chi Kung exercises specifically designed to strengthen the eyes, as well as exercises for the liver.

Reiki treatment
Concentrate treatment on the eyes and
head, and on the liver to clear toxins.

1 Place your hands over the eyes
using Position 1b (see page 221).

2 Cradle the head, using Position 3c
(see page 224).

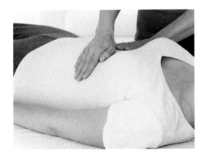

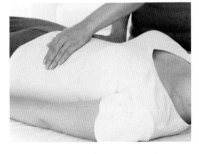

3 Treat the liver by using Position 6
(see page 228).

4 Use Position 7 (see page 229) to
complete treatment of the liver.

Anxiety

Most people experience a certain amount of anxiety, but when it becomes a dominant response to living it is unhealthy. Anxiety is a broad term that covers a range of emotions from mild unease to intense fear. The root causes of anxiety vary from learned responses to specific situations to unconscious internal conflicts, or a physiological response to events as a result of overstimulation of the central nervous system.

The condition produces a broad spectrum of symptoms ranging from the mild to the severe. Many people having an anxiety attack may experience palpitations, chest pain and constricted breathing, and feel as if they are having a heart attack. Other general symptoms are nausea, sleeplessness, diarrhoea and loss of appetite combined with irritability, irrational fears and extreme pessimism. Orthodox methods of treating the condition are psychotherapy or counselling and, for some symptoms, medication.

Emotionally, anxiety represents a sense of being alone in the world. A person with anxiety does not trust the process of living and has lost faith that the Universe always provides solutions to all situations.

Complementary treatments

- BACH FLOWER REMEDIES Use Rescue Remedy when you feel anxiety building up or when having a panic attack.

- EXERCISE Practise yoga or Chi Kung regularly to reduce stress.

- MEDITATION Regular meditation on connection to the Universe or to God or whatever you consider to be the creative energy of the Universe, will reduce any feelings of separation.

Reiki treatment

This sequence balances the adrenals, which increase adrenalin production when we are anxious and become quickly exhausted.

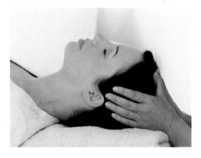

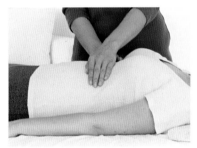

1 Place the heels of your palms on the crown of the head, fingertips pointing down in front of the ears.

2 Treat the front of the body, starting with Position 6 (see page 228) at the solar plexus.

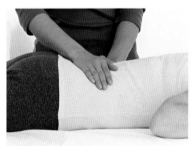

3 Work down to cover the liver, spleen, pancreas and stomach using Position 7 (see page 229).

4 On the back, treat the adrenals and kidneys using Position 14 (see page 236).

Fatigue

Fatigue is a common condition in the modern world that is characterized by more than simply feeling tired. It is a collection of symptoms that includes tiredness along with lethargy and lack of motivation. Fatigue is caused by sleeplessness, and therefore may accompany insomnia, but it is caused by a poor diet as well. It may also be caused by underlying disorders such as anaemia, depression, anxiety and cancer; therefore persistent fatigue should be investigated by a doctor.

It may be treated by a change in diet, adding more foods that are rich in iron, folic acid and Vitamin B12. These can also be taken as supplements. Rest is also important. Fatigue is a sign that we have done too much and as a result are out of balance. We have probably given too much time to activities that require us to expend energy, such as work, and have not taken the time to restore ourselves with activities that nourish us in body, mind and spirit, such as meditation, painting, reading and taking care of our bodies in a loving way. As a result, our minds and bodies never get to relax fully, and we become depleted of energy. Fatigue is a message from mind, body and spirit to change your lifestyle and find balance in your life.

Complementary treatments

- AROMATHERAPY Have regular aromatherapy massages to stimulate the body and relax it.

- EXERCISE Gentle exercise such as walking, yoga and Chi Kung will help release mental and physical stress.

- MEDITATION Use meditation to release mental stress.

Reiki treatment

As with all conditions, it is best to give a full treatment if possible, but you can focus on areas that are particularly affected by stress to help fatigue.

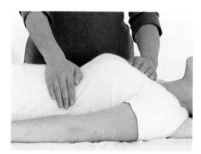

1 Place one hand over the thymus and the other hand over the spleen on the left hand side of the body.

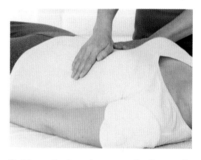

2 Place the hands across the front of the body, covering the solar plexus using Position 6 (see page 228).

3 Move your hands one hand-width down to Position 7 (see page 229).

4 Treat the adrenals and kidneys on the back using Position 14 (see page 236).

Headaches

Headaches are caused by constriction of the blood vessels in the lining of the brain and by tension in the scalp. Different types of pain may be experienced, varying from a dull, throbbing ache to the deep, sharp type.

The main cause of headaches is usually stress or tension caused by emotional factors; or they may be caused by environmental factors, such as poor lighting or diet. Most headaches pass quickly, and can be treated with painkillers, but persistent headaches may point to an underlying condition and you should seek medical treatment for them.

Emotionally, a headache is a symptom of an overloaded mind.

Reiki treatment

Treat the head and follow with stress-affected areas such as the solar plexus.

1 Treat the head. Start by using Position 1b (see page 221).

Complementary treatments

• AROMATHERAPY Rubbing lavender oil onto the temples reduces pain and promotes relaxation.

• MASSAGE An Indian head massage or a full body massage will help to work on the root causes of the headache.

2 Continue treating the head, using Position 2a (see page 222).

3 Treat the spleen, liver and stomach. Start with Position 6 (see page 228).

4 Contune treating the area by moving into Position 7 (see page 220).

5 Treat the adrenals and kidneys on the back using Position 14 (see page 236).

Insomnia

Insomniacs find it difficult to fall asleep or to stay asleep. Most people experience insomnia briefly at some point in their lives, usually in response to a stressful situation. However, for some people it turns into a chronic condition that may last for years. The causes of insomnia are frequently underlying conditions such as depression and anxiety, and drug users are also likely to experience it during withdrawal. It may be related to lifestyle factors such as shift work, excessive caffeine intake and lack of exercise.

Insomnia is usually treated by establishing a more regulated lifestyle including a regular time for going to bed, but insomnia caused by depression may be more difficult to treat and require a number of approaches, including medication and counselling or psychotherapy.

Chinese medicine and other healing methods see insomnia as indicating a weakness in the liver and gallbladder, and treatment focuses on these organs. Emotionally, a person with insomnia may be feeling unable to surrender or be vulnerable, which is what we are when we are sleeping. They are also unable to trust life and fear for their survival.

Complementary treatments

- AROMATHERAPY As well as having aromatherapy massages, you can use a variety of oils at home either in the bath or to scent the bedroom. Consult an aromatherapist about the oils that will work best for you. Lavender is the standard oil for relaxation, and you could also try patchouli and benzoin, both of which are grounding.

- EXERCISE Some form of daily exercise such as walking will help with relaxation.

- HERBALISM Drink herbal teas such as camomile and rosehip to calm and soothe the nerves.

Reiki treatment

These positions are also ideal for self-treatment of insomnia. For maximum benefit, give treatments just before bedtime, If possible.

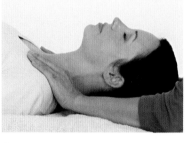

1 Place your hands in Position 1a (see page 221) to tune into the recipient's energy flow.

2 Move into Position 1b (see page 221) by lowering your hands onto the recipient's face.

3 Place your hands in Position 2a (see page 222).

4 Gently move into Position 3a (see page 223), rolling the head to the right.

5 Move your hands into Position 3b (see page 224).

6 Slowly roll the head back to the centre, using Position 3c (see page 224).

7 If you have Second Degree Reiki, move into Position 4a (see page 225) and draw Symbols 1 and 2 on the forehead.

8 Keeping your left hand in place, move your right hand to lie across the forehead in Position 4b (see page 226).

9 Gently slide your hands from under the head, as in Position 4c (see page 226).

10 Place your hands one behind the other beneath the chest area, as in Position 6 (see page 228).

11 To finish, slide your hands into Position 7 (see page 229). It is likely that the person will be deeply relaxed, a state that is restorative.

PART 9
Reiki and other therapies

Acupuncture

Acupuncture is one of the oldest healing methods in the world and is one of the best-known components of Traditional Chinese Medicine (TCM). It works by stimulating specific points on the meridians (see pages 102–105) using very fine, metal needles to pierce the skin. This is not as painful as it sounds. The needles are then manipulated manually by the acupuncturist, or a small electrical current may be passed through them.

The aim of acupuncture is to bring the elements of Yin and Yang into a state of balance. Yin is characterized by cold, passive energy and femaleness, while Yang is hot, active energy associated with maleness. When Yin and Yang are not balanced, blockages in the flow of *Ki* around the meridians occur, and these then manifest as disease. The insertion of the needles removes the blockages.

Acupuncture is now widely used by orthodox medical practitioners as well as those working in complementary practices, and also by many physiotherapists.

Acupuncture is used to treat a wide range of conditions, and has proved to be particularly effective for back pain and pain control in general. It is sometimes used to relieve nausea following chemotherapy and has also helped some people to free themselves from addictions such as smoking and drugs.

Acupuncture and Reiki

Alternating Reiki treatments with acupuncture will not reduce the effectiveness of either. Indeed, the Reiki will enhance the acupuncture by supporting the removal of blockages in the meridians.

Caution

Although there have been very few cases reported of adverse reactions to acupuncture, there are some basic guidelines you should observe.

First, ensure that the acupuncturist is properly trained and has certificates to prove it. The more evidence they can give you of the breadth of their experience, the more likely you are to get an effective treatment. Often personal recommendation is the best way to find an acupuncturist, and there are also professional associations that will help you to find one in your area.

You should also make sure that the acupuncturist uses disposable needles in sealed packets.

RIGHT Acupuncture helps to remove blockages in the meridians, allowing the *Ki* to flow with ease again.

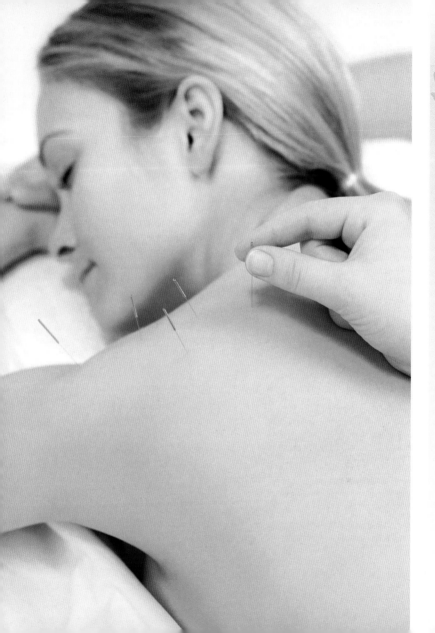

Aromatherapy

Aromatherapy is an ancient art, but the modern practice of using distilled oils for healing was developed in the 1920s by French chemist René-Maurice Gattefossé. He had a perfume laboratory and one day, having burned himself, he plunged his arm into the nearest available cold liquid, which happened to be lavender oil. He then observed that the pain decreased, the burn healed more quickly than usual and there was little or no scarring. This prompted him to investigate the healing properties of other plant and fruit oils.

Aromatherapy involves the treatment or prevention of disease with essential oils. These can be used in a number of ways. You can add them to your bath or add them to a base oil and massage in; both these methods work on absorption of the oils through the skin. The other method of use is inhaling them, either by using an oil burner or by adding them to hot water and inhaling the steam. Using them in the bath or inhaling them are the most popular methods of home use of oils, while aromatherapists tend to combine their use with massage.

Orthodox medicine does not give much credence to aromatherapy other than to accept that it promotes relaxation. This attitude is based on the fact that it has proved very difficult to conduct studies on it that are acceptably

Useful oils to have at home

If you are buying oils to use at home, beware of cheap brands as they will not bring any benefits and are only useful as room scenters. You should always look for oils that are of a therapeutic grade. The oils vary in price – those made from commonly available plants, such as lavender or pine, are significantly cheaper than rarer ones, such as pure rose oil.

- **Anti-bacterial** – rosemary, tea tree
- **Anti-depressive** – lavender, rose
- **Anti-fungal** – lavender, juniper
- **Anti-inflammatory** – eucalyptus
- **Anti-viral** – lemongrass, sandalwood, thyme

ABOVE Essential oils stimulate parts of the brain linked to emotions, each working to support positive changes.

scientific for the medical community. Physiologically, there are two possible explanations for how it works and why it does heal both physical and emotional conditions. The first theory is that the aromas stimulate the limbic system in the brain. This is linked to the olfactory system and supports the emotions. The other explanation is that the plant essences have a pharmacological effect, just as they do in herbalism.

Aromatherapy is safe, although caution must be taken during pregnancy.

Aromatherapy and Reiki

Aromatherapists frequently combine Reiki with a massage, because the two complement each other by intensifying the effects of both.

Massage

Massage is the manipulation of the soft body tissues. Massage can be used on every body part from head to foot, and it focuses on muscles, tendons, connective tissues and the lymphatic system.

Massage has been adopted by orthodox medicine for a wide range of physical conditions involving the muscles and joints, and it is also valued for its effects on stress, depression and anxiety.

Types of massage

A bewildering array of massage types is available now. Some of the most commonly found are described here.

Swedish massage

One of the best known and widely available types, this is based on five types of strokes. It is effective in treating stiffness in the joints.

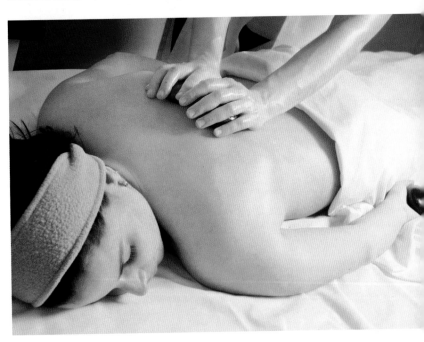

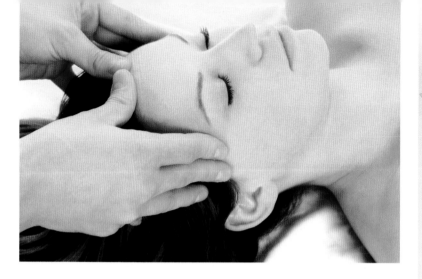

LEFT Massage is well-established as an effective form of treatment for a wide range of physical conditions.

ABOVE Indian head massage is very popular and helps to balance the chakras.

Shiatsu

A Japanese method of massage that uses thumb pressure to work along the meridians, in a similar way to acupressure. Part of the method also includes stretching the limbs. This method is very suited to treating the emotional root cause of physical conditions.

Thai massage

Thai massage treatments are generally longer than the average massage treatment. They are based on yoga, and during the treatment the body will be manipulated into yoga-like postures. As in shiatsu, thumb pressure is also applied to specific points. It is very useful for releasing energy blocks and restoring balance.

Bowen therapy

Developed by Tom Bowen, this technique involves a rolling movement over the muscles, tendons and joints. It is beneficial for releasing muscle tension and improving lymphatic flow.

Indian head massage ('champissage')

This type focuses on the head, face and shoulders, and releases tension in all the muscles in that area. Its primary use is to balance the chakras.

Massage and Reiki

In a similar way to that of aromatherapy, Reiki combines very effectively with massage. The hands can channel the energy while also delivering the massage.

Bach flower remedies

This range of remedies was developed by Dr Edward Bach (pronounced 'Batch'), a medical practitioner who at one point had a successful Harley Street practice. His interest in homeopathy and his natural gift as a healer led him to seek purer alternatives to the traditional homeopathic medicines that are based on treating disease with the products of that disease, often described as 'treating like with like'. The philosophy behind his system is one of treating the mental and emotional states of the patient, and that when these states are unblocked the physical symptoms that manifest as a result of the emotions are healed.

Using his intuition, he spent his springs and summers searching for and preparing the plant remedies that affect each emotional state, until he had created a set of 38 remedies that treated each of them. The remedies are made by two methods: floating the blooms in pure water for several hours, or boiling them for half an hour. They are then combined with pure brandy to preserve them on a 50/50 ratio.

A practitioner will be able to advise you on the remedy, or combination of remedies, for your specific emotional state. A method I have used successfully is to use a pendulum over a chart of the remedies with the intention of selecting the appropriate remedy for myself, or for other people that I have also been treating with Reiki. The Bach remedies are very useful for treatment of children as well as adults, and there are no known adverse effects.

Taking the remedies

You can either drop them straight onto the tongue, or dilute 4 drops in 30 ml water and drink it, four times a day.

Useful remedies at home
- **Elm** – when feeling overwhelmed by responsibility
- **Gorse** – when experiencing a sense of hopelessness or despair
- **Olive** – for exhaustion following mental or physical effort
- **Rescue Remedy** – the most famous of the Bach products, this was developed by Dr Bach as an emotional first-aid kit based on his observation of the typical emotional reactions to crisis
- **Star of Bethlehem** – used to treat shock

RIGHT Flower remedies have no known adverse effects, making them ideal for children.

Bach ®

BACH

riginal

inapis arvensis in a

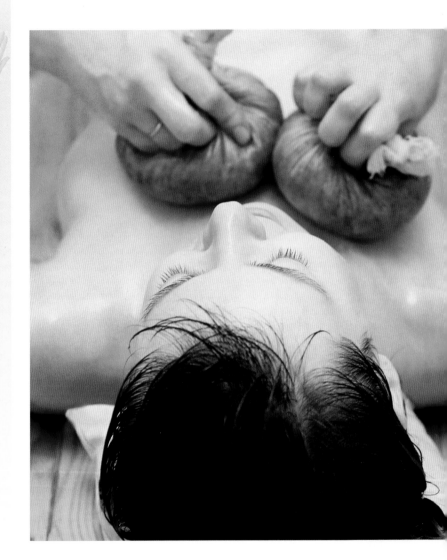

Ayurveda

Ayurvedic medicine is an ancient system that comes from India and is still widely used there. In recent years, it has become more popular in the West, making it easier to find practitioners and training courses. Rooted in the philosophy of the Vedas, Ayurveda takes a holistic approach to treatment. It has eight branches, or specialities, similar to the divisions in Western medicine.

The system is based on the concept that optimum health relies on the balance of three *Doshas* called Vata, Pitta and Kapha. Each person has a dominant *Dosha*, but all three need to be in balance. The Ayurvedic physician will assess you physically and emotionally, and take a series of pulses, to determine your dominant *Dosha* and what is not in balance. They treat an imbalance with a range of herbal remedies and may recommend following a diet based on the principle that certain foods calm or irritate each of the *Doshas*. They also use massage treatments.

Ayurveda and Reiki

Ayurvedic and Reiki treatments combined can heal conditions rapidly and prevent recurrence for many people.

LEFT Ayurveda is a complete system of medicine with a variety of treatments from dietary advice to massage.

The three *Doshas*

The *Doshas* are similar to the idea of 'body humours', which were a feature of early Western medicine.

Vata

Associated with the elements of air and ether, Vata governs breathing, muscle movement and the heartbeat, among other things. People with a dominant Vata are creative, slender, excitable, impulsive and prone to headaches, hypertension and problems with the nervous system when Vata is imbalanced.

Pitta

Associated with water and fire, Pitta governs digestion, metabolism and intelligence, among other things. People with a dominant Pitta have sharp intellects and a strong, medium build, are competitive and easily angered, and prone to ulcers, skin rashes, insomnia and anaemia when Pitta is imbalanced.

Kapha

Associated with water and earth, Kapha governs the physical structure of the body and the lubrication of the joints. People with a dominant Kapha are slow in speech and movement, of heavy build, easy-going and prone to sinusitis and respiratory problems when Kapha is imbalanced.

Yoga

One of the advantages of yoga is that, as with Reiki, it is a practice you can do yourself. Added to this, the yoga postures not only work on the energy body, but also stretch the physical body, ensuring that mobility can be maintained for longer as you age. Although yoga may appear to be too strenuous for those with musculoskeletal problems, an experienced teacher can adapt the postures to include them in classes, or run ones specially for people who need a much gentler form of yoga. Yoga originates from ancient Indian texts that describe the philosophy behind the practice and the postures (*Asanas*), breathing practices and forms of meditation.

Yoga works to balance the chakras as the postures aim to free up the movement of *Ki* around the body. This is called *Prana* in the yoga tradition. Through a set of postures that work the entire body, the *Kundalini* energy stored at the base of the spine rises up through each chakra until it reaches the crown chakra. Being able to bring the energy up to the crown leads to *Samadhi*, which is when we experience unity with the universal spirit.

Hatha yoga

The form of yoga most commonly practised in the West is Hatha yoga, which is based on adopting physical postures. There are several forms, the three best-known ones being Iyengar, Ashtanga and Sivananda. A popular new form is Bikram, which is very physical and performed in rooms kept at high temperatures to encourage sweating.

Iyengar

This form of yoga focuses on correct body alignment for each posture, and uses a variety of props such as straps and blankets to enable the student to achieve advanced poses.

Ashtanga

A very active form of yoga that is challenging for the beginner, it focuses on the strength and flexibility of the student and on all the movements being synchronized with the breath.

Sivananda

This type of yoga focuses on the working the solar plexus area. It combines the use of postures with breathing techniques, diet and meditation.

RIGHT Yoga balances the chakras and improves the flow of *Ki* around the body.

Chi Kung

Like acupuncture, Chi Kung is one of the pillars of Traditional Chinese Medicine (TCM). The name means 'energy cultivation'. It is similar to yoga in that it uses body movement and breathing to improve the flow of energy around the body, but it is less extreme in its body postures and therefore may be more suitable for those of limited mobility, or people who enjoy slower, more meditative movements.

The origins, theory and practice of Chi Kung can be found in *The Yellow Emperor's Classic of Internal Medicine*, a medical text written around the 3rd century BCE. This textbook is still used today by practitioners of TCM, but it is only in the past 20–30 years that Chi Kung has had a resurgence in China, and many millions of all ages practise it daily there. For this reason, it only appeared even more recently in the West, but is now growing in popularity, along with Tai Chi, which is a related practice but uses longer series of steps in its exercises.

By using gentle stretching exercises combined with breathing techniques and visualization, Chi Kung balances the *Chi*. Its primary aim is to prevent disease and promote longevity.

LEFT Chi Kung improves the flow of energy around the body and is suitable for people with limited mobility.

The Taoist tradition

There are many styles of Chi Kung, stemming from five main traditions: Taoist, Buddhist, Confucian, martial arts and medical. Of these, it is the Taoist philosophy that forms the roots of Chi Kung. This philosophy has an organic view of the world, which centres around the need to be in harmony with the Tao. The Tao is something that is transcendent and cannot be explained – it just *is*. Chi Kung is a path to that state of harmony that is 'being in the Tao'.

Chi Kung and Reiki

Reiki practitioners will find Chi Kung easy to practise because of prior knowledge of working with energy. Practising Chi Kung improves your understanding of the way Reiki works from a different perspective, and therefore enhances your ability to work with it. You can also do distance healing with Chi Kung once you have been practising it for some time. I used to exchange distance healing with my Chi Kung teacher – I used Reiki and she used Chi Kung. I could feel the energy just as intensely as if she had been sending Reiki. It may take longer to achieve this with Chi Kung, but it also points to the fact that the symbols are simply tools as we now know Usui intended them to be.

Crystal therapy

Throughout history, crystals and gems have been used for therapeutic purposes. They are once again extremely popular, and many people buy them not just for their healing powers but also for their beauty. As with plants, food and colours, each gem or crystal has an energy vibration unique to its type, and this can be utilized to balance energy.

Crystals need to be cleansed before use, and at regular intervals, and you should consult a book such as *The Crystal Bible* for information on this and on the properties of all the various types of crystals. Whether you buy your crystals in their original rough state, or after having been cut and polished, does not affect their power, so it is entirely a matter of personal preference.

Crystals can be used in various ways. Chakra therapists often place them on the body, using a different crystal for each chakra. In *The Chakra Bible*, Patricia Mercier gives detailed information on the appropriate crystals to use for each chakra that will activate, calm or balance them.

Popular crystals

The most popular types of crystals are ones from the quartz family. The structure of these stones makes them more effective at holding healing energies. Amethyst and rose quartz are widely available.

Amethyst

This crystal is thought to be a powerful aid to spiritual advancement that promotes feelings of divine love, intuition and creative inspiration, as it works with the pineal and pituitary glands and right-brain activities. Physically, it supports the endocrine and immune systems.

Rose quartz

Often referred to as the 'love stone', this delicate pink crystal promotes forgiveness and compassion and restores emotional balance by helping us release anger and fear. Physically, it works with the spleen, kidneys, heart, circulation and reproductive system.

Crystals and Reiki

Although the use of crystals is not part of the original Reiki system, many teachers and practitioners now use them as an addition to treatments. Reiki practitioners using crystals often make crystal grids, which they then place in the room they use for giving treatments. The crystals are charged with Reiki and are thought to amplify the Reiki energy. Details about how to make these can be found in Penelope Quest's book *Reiki for Life*.

RIGHT The popularity of crystals is both based on their beauty and on their ability to alleviate various conditions.

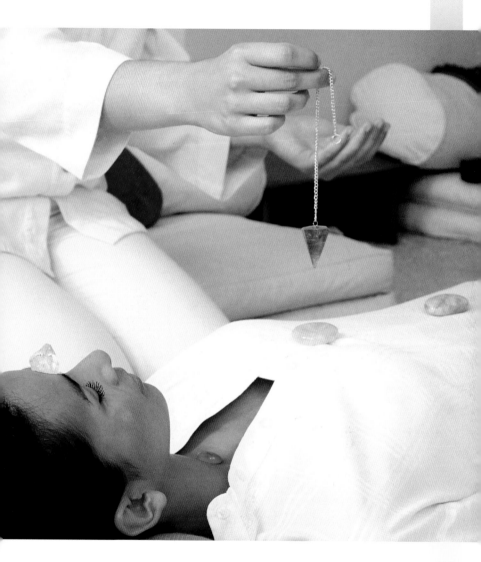

Colour therapy

Evidence of the use of colour as a form of holistic therapy has been found in ancient texts from India, China and Egypt. The principles of the practice are that colour is formed from light of varying wavelengths, and as such it is a form of energy that affects living cells. Used correctly, these different wavelengths, that is different colours, can be used to heal any condition of the body, mind or spirit, and can be safely combined with both orthodox medicine and alternative therapies such as Reiki. Colour therapy does not, however, directly treat the condition, but instead treats the energy block or imbalance that manifests as a physical disease.

The most common methods colour therapists use for their work are placing coloured silks on the body, directing coloured light onto the body, and meditating with colour. They will also analyze your personal colour preferences, as these are thought to reveal imbalance in certain areas. They will then recommend ways you can incorporate these colours in your life to restore balance.

BELOW Aura Soma treatments have been shown to be especially effective for releasing emotional blocks.

Colour	Qualities
Red	Energizing and enhances the circulation of blood. When a person is agitated, this colour should be avoided.
Orange	Works to support the sacral chakra, which is associated with relationships, sexuality and creativity. It is useful for treating the spleen and the kidneys.
Yellow	Connected with the solar plexus, this colour activates the nervous system and is beneficial for skin conditions.
Green	Associated with the heart, this colour is calming and acts as a cleanser for the entire physical body.
Turquoise	This colour supports conditions associated with the throat chakra, and is also used to heal acute infections. Emotionally, it supports communication with others.
Blue	This calming colour is frequently used for pain relief and sleep problems. It is also thought to aid spiritual growth.
Violet	This colour is very beneficial to the eyes, and supports mental and emotional activities such as inspiration and spiritual insight.

Index

INDEX

Acknowledgements

Author acknowledgements Thanks to my family and friends who have accompanied me on my journey with Reiki, to all those teachers and writers around the world who have inspired me and to everyone at Godsfield who has worked on producing this book. May you all be blessed.

Executive Editor Jessica Cowie
Senior Editor Lisa John
Executive Art Editor Mark Stevens
Designer Beverly Price, One2Six Creative
Production Controller Linda Parry
Picture Researcher Ciaran O'Reilly

Commissioned Photography © Octopus Publishing Group Limited/Ruth Jenkinson
Other Photography:
AKG F. Kunst & Geschichte 55;
Alamy Adrian Sherratt 386; Captured Sight 305; Geoffrey Kidd 377; JTB Photo Communications, Inc. 20;
JUPITERIMAGES/ Comstock Images 32; Marc Hill 263; Matthew Mawson 123; Radius Images 259; RubberBall 260;
The London Art Archive 41;
Ancient Art & Architecture Collection 42;
Corbis UK Ltd Sakamoto Photo Research Laboratory 29; Image Source 67; Luca Tettoni 385;
Fotolia Nikki Zalewski 187;
Getty Images Image Source 84, 373; Jerome Tisne 271; Kei Uesugi 269; Marcy Maloy 290; Tom Grill 146;
istockphoto.com 171; Amanda Rohde 71; blaneyphoto 274; Emmanuelle Bonzami 31; Kateryna Govorushchenko 19;
Lise Gagne 188; Rolf Weschke 59; Sami Suni 309; Sonyae 278;
Jupiterimages Burke/Triolo Productions 83;
Karipaulus.com 50;
Masterfile 284;
Octopus Publishing Group Limited Frazer Cunningham 101, 161; Peter Myers 137; Ruth Jenkinson 56, 72, 75,
107, 143, 145, 200, 208, 243, 244, 381, 382; William Reavell 178;
Photolibrary Matthew Wakem 49; Mel Yates 115;
Royalty-Free Images 11, 289, 64, 68, 285;
Shutterstock Amy Nichole Harris 27; Joe Gough 167; Konstantin Tavrov 191; Monkey Business Images 277;
murata-photo com 168; niderlander 378; Paul Cowan 199; velora 133; Yanik Chauvin 371, 374, 375.